IF YOU LOVE YOUR
YOU'LL LOVE THIS BOOK!
(YOUR CAT WILL LOVE IT, TOO.)

Of course your cat needs your love—but also a lot more.

It needs your understanding—and this book tells how to interpret the meaning of the sounds it makes and its body movements from tongue to tail.

It needs your response—and this book tells how to communicate in ways that your cat understands.

It needs your care—and this book tells how to cope with illnesses, misadventures, occasional mischief, and moments of madcap playfulness.

In short, your cat needs what you need—this utterly captivating guide to giving your cat all it decidedly desires and definitely deserves.

HOW TO TALK TO YOUR CAT

"There's always something new to learn about cats. Useful with an elegant humor. This is a dish of cream of a book."
—Mordecai Siegal,
Pets Editor, HOUSE BEAUTIFUL

"Fresh and witty, serious and funny."
—LOS ANGELES TIMES

Other SIGNET Books You'll Enjoy

How to talk to your

Cat

*Illustrations by
Nancy Lou Gahan*

Patricia Moyes

A SIGNET BOOK
NEW AMERICAN LIBRARY
TIMES MIRROR

Copyright © 1978 by Patricia Moyes

SIGNET TRADEMARK REG. U.S. PAT. OFF. AND FOREIGN COUNTRIES
REGISTERED TRADEMARK—MARCA REGISTRADA
HECHO EN CHICAGO, U.S.A.

SIGNET, SIGNET CLASSICS, MENTOR, PLUME, MERIDIAN AND NAL
BOOKS are published by The New American Library, Inc.,
1633 Broadway, New York, New York 10019

First Signet Printing, March, 1979

4   5   6   7   8   9   10   11

PRINTED IN THE UNITED STATES OF AMERICA

CONTENTS

CHAPTER ONE

HOW IT ALL STARTED

Nobody knows precisely when *Felis domestica* took its place in human households, but it is certain that tame cats were prized and even revered in Egypt and India more than five thousand years ago. It is likely, however, that the association between men and cats goes back much farther, into the early days of human civilization.

Cave paintings and carvings of cats have been found dating back to the Paleolithic period. It is true that these may be wild rather than domestic cats, although they bear a remarkable resemblance to ancient Egyptian cats, who in turn look very much like our modern oriental breeds. It is clear from these prehistoric representations that the cats were accurately and affectionately observed by the ancient artists; but because their bones have not turned up, like those of dogs and cattle, in the oldest kitchen middens of the cave dwellers, some authorities maintain that the cats were not domesticated.

Personally, I do not think that this necessarily follows, as all statements about that primitive era must be largely conjecture. The absence of bones proves that cats were not eaten and probably that they did not die in the human dwelling. This would not be surprising. Most pet cats today do not die a natural death; they are killed by veterinarians to put an end to a painful illness or a meaningless life, and their owners are with them up to the end. Left to themselves, however, cats who are dying will seek solitude. If this is true today, when they are so much a part of the human family, it must surely have been an even more prevalent trait in that far-off epoch, when the idea of feline-human friendship was in its infancy. To me, the evidence, admittedly scanty, suggests that contact between men and cats came very early and that it was probably the cats who made the first overtures.

After all, cats had no obvious usefulness to primitive man. They could not be trained to assist in the hunt, like dogs, nor to haul and transport, like horses. In fact, they really could not be trained at all. On the other hand, man, with his warm fires and ready supply of food, was clearly useful to cats. So the cats moved into the caves and were tolerated and finally welcomed by their new friends for the simple reason that they (the cats) continued to indulge in their favorite pastime of killing rats and mice. The cats, of course, were never trained for this activity, and they regarded it not as a duty to be performed in bondage, but as a sport to be enjoyed. They must also have realized early on that humans were quite easy to train, for they have been at it ever since.

Cats reached their peak of pampered popularity in the ancient kingdoms of Egypt and Siam. Ownership of the breed now known as the Siamese cat was the exclusive prerogative of royalty until 1884, when the first pair was brought to England, an unprecedented gift from the king of Siam to the British consul general. It is said that the Siamese people were greatly dismayed when the cats left the country, believing that their departure presaged the downfall of the kingdom.

The privileged position of Egyptian cats deteriorated around two thousand years ago with the arrival of the Romans, but up until then, they enjoyed a remarkably high social status. Herodotus, the Greek traveler and historian, assures us that the penalty for killing a cat in Egypt was death and that it was forbidden to export cats for sale. On the other hand, seafaring Egyptian merchants often took their cats with them on trading voyages abroad, and it is thought that these traveling salescats were the direct ancestors of our modern domestic cats.

Bast, the Egyptian cat goddess, is far and away the most attractive of ancient deities. Her rites were celebrated with music and dancing, merry parties, and river trips. She was considered the goddess of well-being, prosperity, fertility, and maternity. In many statues, she is shown as a cat-headed woman, with adorable kittens playing at her feet. The aspects of health and prosperity are logical when you consider that cats destroyed disease-bearing rodents and also protected precious granaries from nibbling raiders. And anybody who has known a cat will understand the light-hearted, antic side of Bast.

Cats in Egypt were not only worshiped; they were loved. Families spent good money to have their pets mummified after death and buried in small, decorated coffins. Many statuettes and paintings of Egyptian cats show them wearing gold necklaces and earrings. I was reminded of this when my husband, a self-professed noncat person, used to play for hours with our first Siamese kitten, festooning her with golden chains and bracelets from my trinket box. She loved it, and he seriously discussed having a golden collar made for her.

Not until the appropriately named Dark Ages did people in Europe turn their backs on their enchanting feline friends and develop a superstitious fear of them. I am afraid that medieval Christianity, with its paranoid fear of a return to the old religion, must bear a heavy responsibility for the horrors of cruelty and persecution that took place. Cats, especially black cats, had figured in some pagan fire and fertility ceremonies and were also regarded as guardian spirits for human households in pre-Christian times. As a consequence, although cats had been valued and even loved during the first thousand years of Christendom, when the great witchcraft scare swept Europe around A.D. 1000, they came to be regarded as witches' familiars and even as embodiments of the devil himself. They were subjected to hideous and completely undeserved persecution. The sweet kittens of Bast were burnt alive, hung, drowned, and disemboweled. It is hardly surprising that they and their descendants developed the habit of selecting their human companions with some care. As a result, they acquired a reputation for aloofness and independence.

All over the world, there are ancient legends about the cat, and all reflect the qualities that we recognize in our own pets: loyalty, dignity, playfulness, and cleanliness. Not one suggests that the cat is cold natured and independent of human beings. The stories tell of cats protecting people and property, remaining steadfastly on guard for impossible lengths of time, foretelling storms at sea and guiding boats to safety, bringing help to benefactors who had fallen on hard times, watching over babies. All these charming tales stem from the era before the Dark Ages, when cats were everybody's friends. Rudyard Kipling, reflecting the post-Dark Ages image, created a haunting but misleading picture when he wrote: "I am the Cat that walks by himself, and all places are alike to me." This is rubbish. People and places are the most important things in the lives of cats. After all, didn't they take the first steps towards domesticating us?

One of the most significant of those steps happened when cats started talking to people. Nobody knows when this occured, but it is a self-evident (and often overlooked) fact that cats do not communicate vocally with each other. Only in the exchanges that accompany courtship or fighting and the gentle crooning of mother-to-kitten talk do cats make noises to each other. Interfeline conversation is carried on by visual and tactile means. Tails, ears, whiskers, and paws all carry messages that, with a little practice, you can learn to interpret. We will talk more about this body language in Chapter Five. Meanwhile, it is worth considering that the welcoming chirrups, demanding miaows, and affectionate mews are directed exclusively towards human beings and can only have been developed as a deliberate method of communication.

As any observant cat owner knows, each individual cat has a huge vocabulary. Siamese are the most garrulous of cats and have a vocal range wider and more varied than that of most breeds. For this reason, owners of Siamese are usually ready to hold conversations with their cats, and most of them find nothing bizarre in the idea. This has earned Siamese owners a curiously paradoxical reputation as, on the one hand, cat nuts and, on the other, people so discriminating as to have chosen a cat that is not really a cat at all, but more like a dog.

Siamese cats are not at all like dogs. They are more like cats than most cats are, that's all, probably because this breed never suffered the traumatic experience of centuries of torture and ill-treatment. I am extremely fond of dogs, but I have never sat down and conversed with one. (I make an exception of the poodle, who is positively catlike in his responses to people.) At best, a dog will gaze into your eyes and allow you to conduct a monologue or soliloquy, to the accompaniment of his wagging or thumping tail. This, I submit, is not a conversation.

On the other hand, it is perfectly possible to converse with any cat, from prize-winning Siamese to alley tabby. Humans who are slow learners may start with a highly articulate Siamese and progress in time to the more sensitive and difficult business of talking to scared strays. Other people, naturally gifted, can talk to any cat right away. I had to learn from my Siamese, but I think I can now interpret both their strong dialect and the subtler language of other breeds.

The most important thing for any cat owner to realize is the deep need that cats have for human friendship and communication. They were not, after all, dragged from the jungle and trained into submission as useful servants; they left an environment in which they were well equipped to survive and struck a bargain with mankind to the benefit of both parties. They sacrificed their much-vaunted independence in return for warmth, companionship, love, food, and a home. When they are deprived of these things, they withdraw, deeply hurt, and are accused of coldness and ingratitude. The dog, in common with many other animals, is prepared to love anybody who feeds him. The cat is prepared to feed or to starve with anybody who loves him (it's simpler to refer to the cat as "him," but of course, everything applies equally to a female). In England,

a popular name for a pub is The Cat and Fiddle. In bygone and predominantly illiterate times, the inn sign told travelers that they had reached journey's end by a painting, swinging from a post outside the inn, depicting the name graphically. So one saw, and still sees, pictures of a cat playing on a violin, and "Hey diddle-diddle, the cat and the fiddle" became a popular song that is now a nursery rhyme. However, the scholarly view is that the name came over from France with the Norman Conquest and is in fact a corruption into English of *le chat fidèle* ("the faithful cat"). In legend and in fact, cats have proved to be every bit as loyal to their human friends as dogs have; and what is more, they talk to us.

Because cats have developed a whole vocabulary directed entirely towards people, it would seem only civil for us to take the trouble to understand and reply to it. The tone of your voice, a surprising number of actual words, your gestures and caresses will soon put you into direct communication with your cat. This communication can prove useful as well as enjoyable, as a recent experience of my own illustrates.

My husband and I have two Siamese cats: Belinda and her son, Spot. Spot is an unusual name for a cat and calls for a little explanation. When we bought Belinda as a kitten, we decided to breed her once before having her spayed and to keep one kitten for ourselves. She had a happy and uncomplicated pregnancy, and exactly on the predicted day, she produced four kittens at the correct half-hourly intervals, the first arriving at noon and the last at one-thirty. I fed Belinda, changed her bedding, and left her in peace for the afternoon with her new family. At seven o'clock in the evening, when Jim came home from work, we both went to visit Belinda and the kittens. And there she was, in the process of giving birth to a fifth kitten, almost seven hours after the others!

It is hard to say who was more surprised, Belinda or ourselves. When the kitten was finally born and the umbilical cord nipped through neatly, Belinda gave me a meaning look and simply walked away from the newborn kitten to rejoin the other four. She was just too exhausted to cope.

I knew that I must split the sac and get the kitten out at once, or he would drown. Then he had to be rubbed with warm, rough towels until his fur fluffed up, and he started to squeak. When all this had been done, I put him to feed with the others, and fortunately Belinda did not reject him. He was a big male kitten and, unlike the others, not quite perfect physically. He had a dark spot on his back, near his shoulder, and a marked kink in his tail. Inevitably, he was nicknamed Spot; and when the other kittens went off to new homes, he stayed with us. He has always been very specially my cat, as Belinda is Jim's, and the fact that I acted as midwife has seemed to make a bond between us.

From early kittenhood, Spot was very vocal, and he and I developed a system by which I could always tell where he was. If I called his name in a particular two-tone chant, high and low, he would answer me with an unmistakable call, a series of short, urgent miaows. This system has persisted and comes in handy if he gets out of my sight on country walks (we always take the cats with us wherever we can). When I call him, he keeps up his answering call until we are in sight of each other again. Equally, when the cats go out into our small city garden and maybe scale the fence to visit neighbors, they will come back home in response to my special call. Belinda just arrives silently, but Spot answers me as soon as he hears me, and I listen to his voice getting louder and louder as he nears home.

Recently, Jim and I went on a three-week holiday, leaving Belinda and Spot (who are now middle-aged) in the care of a charming young house-sitter, for we were going to an island with quarantine regulations and could not take the cats. We had a splendid vacation and got home on a Sunday morning, having traveled all night, and were suffering from jet lag. We had proposed to spend the day resting, but no such luck. We were met by a tearful cat-sitter. She had not written to us for fear of ruining our holiday, but Spot had been missing for two weeks. He had gone out as usual for a Sunday evening stroll and never came back.

Everything possible had been done. A reward had been offered in a newspaper advertisement, notices had been posted, and neighbors alerted. People had been patrolling the streets, calling him. He did not reappear. At best, he must have been adopted by somebody else. At worst, he must be dead, either having been run over or accidentally shut up in some deserted building to starve.

Jim's attitude was that after two weeks, it was silly to go on hoping. We must just accept the fact that he had gone for good. This I refused to do, although I admit I was pretty downhearted. However, I felt absolutely certain that if he was alive and within earshot, he would hear me calling and answer. So I went out into the streets of Washington and began my two-tone chant, gradually widening the area of my search.

It was a beautiful autumn Sunday, and Georgetown had attracted its usual crowds of sightseers. The traffic was heavy and noisy, and my voice could not have carried far. By the evening, I was almost ready to give up. But as darkness fell and the visitors went home, the streets grew quiet, and I started again.

I was on a residential street about three blocks from home when he answered me. There was no mistaking those short, sharp miaows. I called louder, encouraging him, telling him to find me. At first, I thought that he was trapped in the basement of a house; but as his cries grew in volume, I realized that they were coming from the direction of a big school building on the other side of the road. By our usual process, we homed in on each other in the dark. And suddenly there he was, on the far side of the tall wire fence that enclosed the school's playground. He was terribly thin and frightened, but he was there. We talked a little through the wire, and then I coaxed him to follow me to the gate, where I could see by the street-lamp that he could just squeeze through. Ten minutes later, we were both home.

Of course, we shall never know exactly where he spent those fourteen long days, even though he told us, at almost intolerable length, every detail of his adventure. I am afraid my Siamese is not quite up to interpretation of that order. However, it was abundantly clear that he had become lost and cut off from home and that, although over-to the extreme. My cat, Spot, cannot bear to be left long pact by taking such a long time to come and find him. He needed several days of concentrated affection before he was quite reassured that he had not been deliberately rejected.

To our friends and neighbors (and especially to the house-sitter), it seemed like a miracle that I had been able to find Spot after two weeks. In fact, the miracle took place some seven years earlier, when we evolved our surefire system of communication. That is why I suggest that you start talking to your cat or, better still, to your kitten just as soon as you can. You can't begin too young.

CHAPTER TWO

ACQUIRING A CAT

Many cats and owners come together more or less by chance. You adopt a stray, or vice versa. A friend's cat has kittens, and you are persuaded to take one. Your child falls in love with a fluffy bundle in a pet-shop window. Any way that a cat can come by a good home is to be commended, but it is probably better to go about the business in a rather more deliberate and thoughtful manner.

To start with, what sort of cat do you want? Although every cat is an individual, different breeds do tend to have different characteristics.

If you want your cat to be decorative as well as companionable, you will probably choose an oriental—a Siamese or a Burmese. Because of inbreeding, these cats used to be somewhat delicate

16

and difficult to rear, but the population of seal-point Siamese and Burmese is now large enough and the strains hardy enough to produce beautiful animals with no special health problems. The rarer varieties of Siamese (the blue, lilac, chocolate, and tortie points) may still need a little extra pampering, expecially in very cold weather.

The Siamese is the easiest cat to talk to. In my experience, the males, in particular, are garrulous to the extreme. My cat, Spot, cannot bear to be left out of a human conversation; and if my husband and I are having an earnest discussion about something, Spot will push his way between us, commenting loudly on the matter at hand. I have never known a Siamese who did not have an outstanding personality. They tend to be strong willed, demanding, and very mischievous. They are also intelligent and ingenious, and their love and trust, once given, are boundless. Very few people who have ever owned a Siamese would contemplate another breed.

The Burmese, with his beautiful sable or champagne-colored coat and golden eyes, is an altogether gentler and more manageable creature. He has all the lithe grace of the Siamese but tends to have a sweeter, more biddable nature. Many people consider this a great virtue—but once you have known an opinionated, willful Siamese, the Burmese may seem a little bit too good to be true.

Long-haired cats (Persian, Angoras, Himalayans, and Birmans) are the real aristocrats of the cat world, and they certainly know it. In temperament and even in appearance, they bear a strong similarity to the Pekingese dog. Like him, they are dignified, courageous, and absolutely convinced of their superiority. Their beauty lies, not in streamlined movements and graceful agility, but in their magnificent coats of black, blue, red, cream, or white. And don't forget that these coats need a tremendous amount of work on your part to keep them in condition. Don't consider a long-haired cat unless you are prepared to give it a great deal of your time.

Other exotic breeds (the Abyssinian, the tailless Manx, and the curly haired Rex) are probably only of great interest to serious breeders, although, of course, any cat in the world will make a wonderful pet and friend. However, unless you want a cat that will cost a lot of money and will be a conversation piece, you will probably be happy to settle for an ordinary domestic shorthair: a tabby, tortoiseshell, black, white, or any of the enchanting mixtures of color. And why not? Most "ordinary" cats are not considered ordinary at all by their owners, and although they are not so vocal as orientals, they will develop a considerable vocabulary if encouraged and spoken to from kittenhood.

A very good compromise is to find a half-breed. Mismatings take place in even the best oriental families, and some of the most intelligent and endearing cats are the result of a dash of Siamese or Burmese mingled with a basic tabby strain. What is more, a half-breed kitten will probably cost you nothing; the owner of the purebred mother will be only too delighted to find good homes for the litter.

If you adopt a stray, it goes without saying that the process is a two-way affair. The cat has chosen you as much as you have chosen him. Paul Gallico's delightful book *The Silent Miaow* describes this process from the cat's point of view, and it is not altogether fanciful. What many people do not appreciate, however, is that it is equally important to follow this pattern of mutual selection if you are acquiring a young kitten from a litter.

By the time the kittens are old enough to leave their mother, at about ten weeks, they have developed definite personalities. They also seem to know instinctively that every cat needs one special person, and they recognize that person when he or she comes along. Personally, I get a little impatient with technical cat books that advise you to inspect each kitten clinically and pick the one with the best coat, the brightest eyes, the sturdiest legs, and so forth. You have already decided that you want a cat; to achieve a really satisfactory relationship, you should now leave it up to the particular cat to choose you.

The best way to go about this is to ask the owner to leave you alone in a closed room with just the kittens, not the mother. Sit down on the floor, and watch the kittens play (I could do that all day). When they are quite accustomed to you, join in the game by trailing a piece of string or throwing a small tinfoil ball for them to chase. Before long, one kitten will start to show a particular interest in you. It will start climbing onto your lap, investigating your shoelaces or coat buttons, and generally appearing more intrigued by you than by the game.

This is the moment for some gentle stroking and, above all, talking. Never grab hold of the kitten possessively. Let it make the overtures. By now, both of you will know for sure that you have found each other, and if it is the runt of the litter or has cross-eyes or strange markings, what of it? A relationship that starts out in friendship and trust, rather than in a virtual kidnapping, is almost certain to turn out happily. The kitten will go home with you serenely and not undergo the frightening experience of being wrenched away from its mother and siblings by a stranger and isolated in an unfamiliar environment.

Speaking of isolation, I do recommend that you should seriously consider the prospect of acquiring two kittens rather than one. It is obviously impossible to take a cat with you wherever you go, and I have already pointed out the tremendous need for companionship that all cats share. If you are a member of a large household where somebody is always at home, then a single cat will thrive. But if you are single person or a couple, it is inevitable that the kitten will have to be left alone for considerable periods.

We learned our lesson with Belinda, our first kitten. Whenever we both left the house, she would follow us to the front door, crying pathetically to be allowed to come with us. When we explained that it was really not possible, she would settle herself in a deliberately uncomfortable position as near to the door as possible. When we returned hours later, she would still be there, not having moved a muscle, looking up at us with great, reproachful blue eyes. The result, of course, was that we began to feel guilty every time we left her alone, and it became more and more difficult to enjoy social functions away from home.

The problem was solved by breeding her and keeping one kitten. When she had the whole brood to look after, she was too happy and busy even to notice whether we were around. Then, as the others went off to new homes, Belinda and Spot grew closer together, their relationship changing from mother and kitten to a real companionship. Never again did we find the pathetic waif crouching by the front door, waiting for us to come home. On the contrary, we would come in to find both cats comfortably entwined on the living-room sofa, and our arrival would provoke a positive orgy of mutual licking and ear washing, a demonstration that said clearly, "We are perfectly happy on our own, thank you. If you insist on going out, that's your affair. Don't think we need you." Naturally, we were delighted.

If there are two of you, you will each be able to find a kitten to adopt you as its "special" person. If you are alone, and the kittens have to share you, you should first find your particular cat and then take another from the same litter who seems especially friendly with the one who has chosen you.

In practical terms, such as feeding and grooming, it is really just as easy to cope with two kittens as with one. And from the point of view of the cats' happiness and your peace of mind, it is well worth it.

There remains the question of whether to have male or female animals. Because you will almost certainly be having them neutered, you may feel that the question is academic, but actually each sex has characteristics that persist after the operation. Most female cats are naturally flirtatious and make a great fuss over the men in the family. They are more elegant than the males as a rule and also more mischievous and ingenious, but they are undoubtedly less talkative.

Female cats tend to communicate by gestures and expressions rather than by actual vocalizing. However, when they do speak, it is undoubtedly effective. One small, almost inaudible mew from Belinda on the subject of, say, a late meal or a closed door is more eloquent than a whole tirade on the subject from Spot. The female is the mistress of the silent miaow and of the looks that speak louder than words.

Neutered male cats are usually extravagantly affectionate towards their human friends. They are great talkers and express their need for love and communication more directly than the females do. If they are allowed outside, they are more adventurous and will explore longer and farther than their sisters. They also have a very strong sense of territory and will get into fights with other cats who try to invade their privacy; whereas the females usually content themselves with a display of hissing and tail lashing against the intruder. If you want a cat to cuddle, to use as a hot-water bottle, and to sentimentalize over, then a neutered male is for you.

Unfortunately, unaltered males are usually out of the quesion except for serious breeders. This is a pity, because the male cat in his natural state is a splendid creature. He is gentle and dignified and—given female companionship at home—surprisingly faithful sexually. In a recent experiment with a controlled colony of cats, Dr. Lucile St. Hoyme of the Smithsonian Institute found that pairs formed and lived more or less monogamously within the group. If the male did allow himself to be seduced by another female, his mate would show great distress and displeasure.

Interestingly enough, it was also found that during courtship the male would croon softly and gently to the female, making a noise very much like that used by mother cats to their kittens. This makes an addition to the rare occasions when cats communicate vocally with each other, and it could not be less like the raucous caterwauling that most people associate with mating cats. The ear-piercing screeches, of course, have nothing to do with courtship as such, but are the fighting calls of rival males. In the protected colony, such scrapping was unnecessary, and the true and beautiful love calls made themselves heard. What is more, after the birth of kittens the father would take a great interest in his offspring and would baby-sit to help the female. To apply the word *tomcat* to a promiscuous human male is to do the cat a sad injustice. However, the cat population is too large as it is, and the fewer kittens born to roam alleys and scavenge for food, the better. Which brings us to the question of strays.

Strays may be kittens born to other strays in the murk of urban wildlife. They may also be cats who are lost or who have been abandoned by callous owners who have moved or for some reason have grown bored with their pets. One cat I know was literally picked up by her present owner after he saw her being deliberately thrown out of the window of a moving car. She was pregnant at the time, which may have been why her owner wanted to get rid of her. If, as Blake says, "A Robin Redbreast in a cage/Sets all of heaven in a rage," then I cannot imagine what fearful fate awaits the driver of that car on Judgment Day.

If a stray should turn up at your door, do remember that it may be somebody's dearly loved cat who is lost. By all means, take it in and feed it, but do not automatically assume ownership. Get in touch with the police and your local humane society. Post Found notices on trees and fences around your neighborhood. Scan the Lost column in the local paper. It is as well *not* to advertise your find in the press, however, because unscrupulous people have been known to answer such advertisements in order to get animals to sell to vivisection laboratories. If your stray really is loved and lost, then its owners will be the ones to advertise.

If, after several weeks, there is no sign of any previous owner, then you may safely assume that the cat is yours. This is the moment to take it to the vet for a complete physical checkup and all the inoculation shots that the doctor recommends.

Finally, you may decide to get your pet from the pound or animal shelter. This is certainly the most praiseworthy thing to do, for you will be saving an animal from certain death. It is not, of course, the ideal way to achieve a process of mutual selection, but even in that jailhouse atmosphere, there may well be a coming together of cat and person. A cat from the pound is undeniably yours from the moment you take possession of it, so you can take it straight away for its shots and physical examination.

A cat that has undergone the traumatic experiences leading up to and culminating in incarceration in the pound is apt to be nervous and withdrawn. Don't rush things or expect too much too soon. A cat that has been shut up in a cage by strangers, however well-meaning, may be prejudiced against the entire human race for a while. The best thing is to keep the cat indoors for several days, secure but not under strict restraint. It may run away from you and hide in a remote and inaccessible corner. Never mind. Talk to it,

and provide it with food. Don't chase the cat or
harass it. Basically, cats want to associate with human beings, and it will soon begin experimenting
with you to see if you are trustworthy. Just make
sure that you are.

Many people acquire a kitten, not for themselves, but for their children. Of course, it is an
excellent idea for children to be brought up with
young animals and to learn to love and care for
them, but you should *never* get a kitten (or any
other animal) for a child as a result of a sentimen-
tal impulse or as a surprise present. Children develop genuine and spontaneous enthusiasms, but
they also get bored quickly. A child who wants a
kitten must be made to understand beforehand
that his pet is a living creature, a member of the
family, not a toy; that it is a serious responsibility
to undertake to feed, groom, and look after an animal for the rest of its life; and that, however in-
convenient it may be, there will be no question of
running off to play or go to a movie before the
kitten has been given its dinner.

Of course, no child is a paragon of all virtues;
and with the best of intentions, there will be
lapses. In those cases, you must be prepared to
care for the kitten yourself. Never let the animal
go hungry so that you can say to your child, "Look
what you've done to poor little kitty by forgetting
to feed him." Scold the child, by all means, but
don't take it out on the cat.

It is never a good idea to give a kitten to a very young child. Before the age of four, a child does not really comprehend the difference between a live animal and a toy, nor does he understand the pain and injury that he can inflict by his well-meant but clumsy gestures of affection. If there is already an adult cat in the family when the baby arrives, that is fine. The cat will be able to protect itself easily against any unwanted attentions and will make an excellent playmate for the child. But a kitten is itself tiny and uncoordinated and extremely vulnerable, and it should not be subjected to the rough-and-tumble of the nursery.

However, let us assume that you, the adult, are getting a kitten for yourself. You have visited the

owner of a mother cat and have been selected by
your special kitten. You have put him in a basket
and brought him home. Now is the time to begin
the process of establishing communication.

CHAPTER THREE

FIRST STEPS IN
COMMUNICATION

The very first step in communicating with your kitten is to accustom him to his name. It is best to decide on a name before you get the kitten so that you can begin using it right away. Talk to the kitten on your way home, mentioning his name as often as possible. Baby talking to animals is just as silly as baby talking to babies, so just explain to your kitten what your plans are, where he is going to live, and so on. Now, I'm not saying for a moment that the little creature will understand what you say. But he will be growing accustomed to the sound of your voice, and he will soon cotton on to the fact that the constantly repeated word (his name) is connected with himself.

When you get home, do not let the kitten out of his basket until you are safely inside a room with all doors and windows closed. In spite of all your reassurance, the kitten may be scared. And if he rushes off and hides—well, a tiny kitten can move with incredible speed, and the needle in the proverbial haystack is easier to find than a six-inch bundle of fluff in a largish house.

I speak from experience. When we bought Belinda, my husband and I went together to choose and be chosen, and Belinda instantly picked Jim as her person while quite clearly rejecting me. However, he then had to go back to his office, leaving me to take the kitten home. By the time we arrived, Belinda was furious and dismayed; her chosen person had deserted her. As I opened her basket in the living room, she shot out like an arrow from a bow and completely disappeared. It took me an hour and a half to find her; she had gone to earth underneath an old divan in the back attic. I am pretty sure that if Jim, her person, had brought her home himself, she would not have staged such a demonstration of fright and temper, but just in case this happens to you, I would advise imposing some restraint.

You will, of course, have purchased suitable food and a cat basket before acquiring the kitten. Now is the time to produce a small saucer of food and some warm milk and to introduce the kitten to his bed. He will almost certainly show minimal interest in the basket, and unless you are superhumanly strong minded, he will sleep on your bed for the rest of his life. Still, it's worth a try.

Meanwhile, keep talking. It is not too soon to start on the establishment of a calling code so that your kitten will always come to you when he hears a particular sound. The obvious way to achieve this is to associate the call with food, and you can begin with the very first dish you offer the kitten, I use a high-low call and the words, "All cats!" But what you actually say is not important. It is the pitch of your voice that counts. If you repeat your call every time you feed the kitten, he will very soon learn to come running when he hears those notes.

During this early training process, it is very important always to reward the kitten with a small tidbit if you call him for some other purpose than a regular feed. A kitten who has come scampering to answer a food call only to be grabbed and put into a carrying basket and taken to the vet for an inoculation will soon get disillusioned and will respond to the call only when he knows it is mealtime.

Of course, the ultimate idea is to develop a personal call sign independent of food association, as I have done with Spot. But for the first year or so, you must praise and reward the cat every time he responds. (I nearly wrote "Obeys", but that is not the right word. The process is entirely voluntary.)

I do not believe that it is possible to teach a cat to obey; that is contrary to his nature. Your cat will quickly get to know from the sound of your voice and your obvious displeasure which activities are forbidden, such as tearing up the furniture, stealing food, or knocking small objects off the mantelpiece. However, the fact that he knows these things to be wrong does not necessarily prevent him from doing them. Very few cats will incur your displeasure deliberately and for no reason, but almost all of them will use these unlawful acts either to attract your attention or to protest against what they feel to be injustice or neglect.

For example, on the few occasions when we have to go away for a day or so, leaving the cats at home with no companionship other than a neighbor to feed them twice a day, we can expect to find the furniture in poor shape when we get home. If Belinda is very hungry in the morning and thinks that I am lying too long in bed instead of preparing her breakfast, she will jump onto the bedside table and quite deliberately knock the objects off it one by one with her paw, starting with small things such as pens and eyeglasses, and working up (if necessary) to the reading lamp.

This is just mischief, but if cats are really driven to desperation by loneliness or ill-treatment, they will react by committing more serious crimes, such as stealing food and even, as a last resort, defecating in the house, usually in the bathtub. This is a curious phenomenon that many cat owners have experienced, and it should be regarded, not as wickedness, but as a heartrending cry of despair. Cats, by their nature, are the cleanest of animals. Unlike dogs, they need no house-training; they will use the garden or a cat box quite spontaneously. They also clean up meticulously by burying their excrement with what sometimes seems unnecessary thoroughness. The act of fouling their own home is their most extreme way of crying for help and consolation, of getting your attention at all costs, even if that attention takes the form of anger or punishment.

Let's get back to your new kitten. As well as accustoming him to his name and the food call, these first days are the time for a maximum amount of talking. You will soon get into the habit of discussing things with your kitten, just as if he were a person. When you come into the house, call the kitten by name; and when he comes to you, pick him up, greet him affectionately, and tell him where you have been and what you have been doing. In a very short while, you will find that you do not have to call. He will hear your key in the lock and will come running, mewing urgently, trying to get his account of *his* day in before yours.

We will discuss the actual sounds in Chapter Four, but take it from me that you will quickly come to understand whether the cat has had a boring, exciting, pleasant, or unpleasant time while you were out. A great deal of affectionate body language—writhing round your legs, butting with the head, and purring—combined with a lack of vocal communication usually denotes a bad conscience. Don't be surprised to find something broken or spilled. In this case, it will have been an accident. Cats do not apologize for deliberate naughtiness.

Listening to your cat is as important as talking to it. Cats are sensible and sensitive creatures, and they are hurt if you ignore them when they tell you about their needs and experiences. As always, their reaction when upset is to withdraw and keep quiet. So take a little time, especially if you have been out or away from home, to sit down with your cat or kitten and let him talk to you. Of course, you won't understand any details, but you will be able to catch his mood—happy, bored, excited, cross, or sad. Caress him gently, and reply with such platitudes as: "Did you really?" "And what happened then?" "Yes, you were absolutely right." Your kitten will adore this and become more and more vocal and body expressive. Spot enjoys these talk sessions so much that he has taught himself to perform the seemingly impossible feat of mewing and purring simultaneously. Don't ask me how he does it; I have no idea. I am simply reporting a fact.

On the other hand, Belinda uses body language almost exclusively. This does not mean that she needs less listening to than Spot. Because she is Jim's cat, she prefers to have her talk sessions with him, although she will put up with me if necessary. By her actions, she can convey every bit as much information as Spot does vocally. Incidentally, while I think that our two cats, male and female, in general behave with the characteristics of their sexes, there can be exceptions. Another pair of Siamese whom I know react in precisely the reverse manner, with the female doing all the talking and the male being strong and silent.

All cats who have a loving and trusting relationship with their owners are remarkably sensitive to human moods. If you are depressed, your cat will know exactly how long you need nothing but warm, quiet sympathy and at what moment you are sufficiently recovered to be diverted by an antic display of tricks and mischief. If you are ill, your cat will not leave you except to eat and use his box. If you are pleased and excited, he will join in the fun.

By the same token, you should be aware of your cat's moods. Does he want to play, or does he feel like a quiet talk? Does he want to be picked up and petted, or is he eager to go out adventuring? Is he feeling sorry for himself or on top of the world? He will tell you if you will listen.

Above all, cats need reassurance, especially if you have planned something out of the ordinary and perhaps alarming for your pets, such as a visit to the vet. My husband (who will tell you that he doesn't *really* like cats) once said in a moment of perception, "It must be terrible to be a cat and never make the decisions." Certainly, the decisions are up to you, but at least you can tell the cat about them in advance and explain what is going on.

As soon as I make an appointment at the animal hospital for my cats, I tell them about it. "It'll be next Wednesday. Nothing to worry about. Just a general checkup and a couple of shots." Nevertheless, when the traveling box is brought out for a hospital visit, the cats are extremely reluctant to get into it; whereas if we are headed for the country or the boat, they are eager to be off and will even pack themselves ahead of time to be sure of not getting left behind. The difference in attitude can only be because they have had their destination explained to them.

It would be convenient, sometimes, to pretend that the outing is to be a pleasure trip when in fact it is not. This would eliminate last-minute scufflings under beds to haul out reluctant members of the party. However, we never do it, because it would violate the trust that the cats have in us and we would never get their fullhearted cooperation again.

As a matter of fact, a little while ago, we were off for a country weekend, and I had explained to the cats that we were going to their favorite hotel in the mountains. They jumped happily into their box, and we set off. However, we had an errand to do before leaving town, and so the car turned off the road leading to the country and up the hill in the direction of the animal hospital.

The cats reacted violently. They were out of

their box by then, sitting on my lap with their collars and leads on, while Jim drove, so that they could look out of the window and see just where we were going. There were shouts of protest and great agitation and indignation. I assured them that we really *were* headed for Charlottesville, but not until we were on the westbound road again did they settle down. By contrast, if they know we are going to the hospital, they remain quiet and gloomily resigned, accepting the inevitable. What had them in such an uproar was the suspicion that they had been tricked. As with children, the golden rule when dealing with cats is: Never tell a lie; never break a promise.

I said earlier that it is virtually impossible to teach a cat to obey, but obviously your kitten must be warned to avoid things that might hurt him, such as the hot burners on the kitchen stove, sharp knives, and busy city streets. The way to administer the warning if the kitten is running into danger, is with a sharp, definitive "No!" and a tap on the nose. I cannot emphasize too strongly that you must *never* hit a cat. It will not do the slightest good from a disciplinary point of view and will set back his training disastrously, perhaps forever. On the other hand, the gentle tap on the nose is how the mother cat warns her kittens of potential danger. Even as adults, cats instinctively react to the warning and take notice of it; whereas any sort of corporal punishment will only result in misery and rebellion.

However, the note of displeasure in your voice and the momentary withdrawal of affection will make a deep impression. If the cat has been really naughty, you can allow your disapproval to last for quite a while (say, ten minutes) before you pick him up and caress him and assure him that all is now forgiven. If you have merely been giving a warning against danger, the reassurance should come immediately, for it is very important that your kitten should know from the earliest possible moment the difference between naughtiness and foolhardiness.

On a happier note, play is an excellent form of communication between kittens and their people, and it should be accompanied by talk. Kittens have very different temperaments. Some of them love rough and rowdy games. Belinda was one of these. Even today, as a middle-aged matron, she adores it when Jim throws her through the air to land, bouncing, on the bed. Nobody else, of course, would be allowed to take such a liberty. Spot, on the other hand, has always preferred gentler games and ones calling for less physical agility. A piece of string with an empty cotton spool tied to it, suspended from a chair or doorknob, will keep him happy for hours. If your kitten turns out to have a placid and peace-loving nature, don't ever try to force him into rough games. You will only scare him and lose his trust.

I do advise you not to waste your money on elaborate cat toys. Those cute Disneyesque mice

and rabbits may look appealing to you, but they will not interest your cats. Their favorite toys are the simplest of objects: a piece of string, a ball of tinfoil, a feather. The most important ingredient of the game is the playmate, you. Mind you, I admit that I sometimes get a little tetchy when I realize that for about half an hour Belinda has been sitting there with a grin on her face, watching me chase a piece of tinfoil up and down the stairs. Ah, well, it's good for the figure.

Like children, some cats love music and have a strong sense of rhythm. Of our two, Spot is completely tone-deaf; to him, music is nothing but a noise. Belinda, on the other hand, has loved music since she was a kitten. She will settle on a lap to listen to a concert with obvious enjoyment, and if she is held and rocked in time to the music and gently sung to, she goes into an ecstasy of purring.

So far, we have been talking about establishing the first steps in communication with a kitten newly taken from its mother and without previous relationships with people. But what happens if you adopt an older cat?

If you know the cat's previous owner, you can of course discuss with him or her the methods of communication to which the cat is accustomed. If the ex-owner looks at you as if you are out of your mind, you can take it that the cat has never been spoken to intelligently and that you will have to start from scratch (not, let us hope, literally).

Such a cat will be in somewhat the same state of mind as the cat from the pound, although to a lesser degree. That is, he will presumably have been adequately fed and therefore will not be overly susceptible to food persuasion. He will also be scared and upset by his unfamiliar surroundings and may hide from you or even show genuine hostility at first. He may also try to escape and get back to his old home. As I said earlier, people and places are of paramount importance to cats; and if human friends disappear, the cat will cling desperately to the place he knows. Everybody has heard stories of cats making their way over incredible distances to regain their old homes, and those stories are not exaggerated.

In view of all this, it is best to be firm about keeping your new pet indoors for the first few days and to work hard to convince him that he has found not only a new home but also a new person. As always, the golden rules are patience, gentleness, nonaggression, and talking. It will take longer to establish an initial rapport with an adult newcomer than with a kitten, and at first nothing sophisticated in the way of communication should be aimed at; just try to establish trust and affection. Once this has been done, you can proceed in the same way that you would with a kitten.

In the case of an adult stray, things are quite different. The stray will have taken at least part of the initiative in approaching you, and he will be overjoyed that his advances are reciprocated. He will be eager for affection, although understandably cautious at first. Above all, he will be hungry, and you can start right away associating food with a certain call. You need not worry that he will roam off and leave you. Adopted strays are the most faithful and rewarding of animals, showing unlimited love and loyalty to their human benefactors.

The problem remains of what to do about a stray who wishes to be adopted but whom you simply cannot accommodate. A few years ago, I was adopted by a stray, who undoubtedly was an abandoned domestic pet. Unfortunately, I was unable to take him in for two reasons. My husband would not hear of it, and our two Siamese threatened to tear the poor thing to pieces if he as much as set paw inside the house.

Luckily it happened during a warm summer, and so I was able to make up a bed for Archie, as he was dubbed, outside on our covered porch. He settled down at once, and I fed him and talked to him out there while Belinda and Spot flattened

' their noses against the glass door leading from the living room and spat out their disapproval.

Obviously, that state of affairs could not go on indefinitely. After about ten days of inquiries, reading Lost ads, and papering the neighborhood with notices, it became clear that nobody was going to claim poor Archie. Nor could I abandon my responsibility for him.

First, I tried to find a home for him among my friends, but I was unsuccessful. Then I made contact with a very special local animal society, which is amateur run and lives by a series of miracles. The point about this society is that it guarantees never to destroy a healthy animal entrusted to its care. There are quite a few of these small, invaluable societies around; and if you love animals, I urge you to seek out the one in your neighborhood and support it, either financially or with practical help.

Anyhow, I offered to pay for all Archie's medical expenses, shots and so forth, so that he could be offered for adoption with absolutely no financial strings attached and a certificate of good health in the bargain. The president of the society then took him into her own home temporarily and reported to me that she had never encountered a sweeter or more amenable cat. It seemed that, having decided to trust me, he was prepared to put up cheerfully with whatever provisions I decided to make for his future. A few weeks later, I received snapshots of Archie in his new permanent home in the country, sleeping luxuriously on the lap of his new owner, both of them smiling blissfully.

This may sound like a facile happy-ending story, and I admit that we were all lucky. Nevertheless, it could be repeated more often if people observed certain basic rules about strays. First, don't become involved unless you are prepared to carry the matter through to some satisfactory conclusion. Second, don't, except as a last resort, simply call the police or the pound; if you do, the animal will be taken off to almost certain death. Third, find out who the really dedicated animal lovers are in your area, and seek their help and advice. No matter if you cannot afford financial support for the cat you are rescuing. Give it houseroom, food, and affection for as long as you can; and then, if you cannot keep it yourself, be sure that you pass it on into good hands. Those hands are always there; all you have to do is be willing to look for them.

CHAPTER FOUR

LISTENING TO YOUR CAT

We now come to the process of analyzing the actual sounds that cats make and attaching meanings to them. As I said before, every individual cat has his own vocabulary, so you will have to use these categories merely as guidelines to understanding your particular pet. However, the noises that cats make can be roughly divided into twelve groups. All breeds of cats will use the same basic intonations to convey their meaning, but the Siamese will always be the loudest, lowest-pitched, and easiest to understand. Ordinary domestic cats use a high, almost piping note for communicating with human beings, and your ear has to become attuned to the nuances of your cat's speech.

Alice, in *Through the Looking-Glass*, remarks that kittens, whatever you say to them, always purr. "If they would only purr for yes and mew for no, or any rule of that sort," she says, "so that one could keep up a conversation! But how *can* you talk with a person if they *always* say the same thing?" This shows us that Lewis Carroll, for all his mathematical genius and understanding of children, never bothered to make a study of cats. However, it is true that purring is the sound most characteristic of cats, so we may as well start with that.

The Purr

Purring appears to be an automatic response to certain stimuli connected with sensory experiences. Most people regard the purr as an unmistakable sign of pleasure, but in fact, cats in great pain will also purr. Purring will break out as a result of actual human contact, such as stroking, but it can also be evoked by the stimulation of other senses. The smell of a turkey roasting in the oven, the warmth of a fire in winter, the sound of a much-loved voice, or the clatter of plates as a meal is prepared—all these can make a cat purr. The breathy, rumbling sound is produced from the back of the nose; funnily enough, nobody is sure exactly how it is done. Certainly it does not involve the vocal cords, as demonstrated by Spot, who can purr and mew simultaneously.

Attractive and heartwarming though purring may be, I cannot regard it as a true communication, because it is essentially an involuntary response to a stimulation of the senses from outside. For example, Belinda, like many oriental cats, delights in jumping from a chair or from the ground onto the shoulder of a human friend. When she executes a beautiful, graceful leap and makes a soft, clawless landing, I congratulate and caress her, and she purrs delightedly. Sometimes, however, her jump is less than perfect, her claws come out to steady her, and possibly I am in the middle of some delicate task such as pouring boiling water from a kettle or threading a needle. In such cases I scold her roundly, but still she purrs. It is the sensation produced by leaping and landing that automatically produces the purring.

The nearest that cats come to using the purr for true communication is in the reverse sense. That is, an angry or sulky cat will do its best *not* to purr when stimulated to do so, just as an angry or sulky person will try not to smile, even in the most diverting circumstances. However, persistent stroking will finally produce the purr, just as persistent good humor will finally produce the human smile, although I have known cats to avoid the caress and run away in order to be able to preserve their injured attitude intact.

Purring, then, usually indicates pleasure, but it is not a deliberate sign of affection.

The Welcome

The welcome is the most gratifying sound a cat owner can hear, a genuine, voluntary expression of pleasure. It consists of a series of short, chirruping mews, each running from high to low tonally. If you have been out or away, the welcoming cat will run towards you as you come into the house, with his tail held high and dancing on his tiptoes, crying his welcoming call.

The welcoming chirrup is not only used to greet humans who have been absent. A sleeping cat who wakes to find you beside him will often make the identical sound in a soft, melting tone that is almost like a deliberate purr.

Only a cat that is relaxed, happy, and secure will produce a true welcoming noise. However pleased he may be to see you, a tense or frightened cat will utter a much higher, sharper note.

I cannot stress too much the fact that a cat who communicates with a person and gets no response will very soon become taciturn and withdrawn. Because the welcome is the most open and affectionate of cat noises, it should never be ignored, however busy you may be. If you are really rushed, a quick greeting, a caress, and a promise of more talk later will have to suffice. The important thing is to show your pleasure and appreciation of your cat's initiative and to make him feel loved and wanted and aware of his own personality. Just as tiny specks of coral build up to become a reef or even an island, so each recognition by you of your cat's identity helps to mold his character. Cats of great personality are always found in association with sensitive, cat-conscious people; it is a two-way process of immense mutual benefit.

Let us assume, however, that you are not desperately busy, that your cat has welcomed you home, and that you have a few minutes to devote to him. This is the time for a talk session, as described in Chapter Three. Sit down with the cat on your lap or beside you, stroke him, and ask him, as you would a child, "Well, what have you been doing all day?" He will understand the tone of your voice and the inflection that implies a question, and soon he will start on his tale.

Information

The informative mew is quite different from the chirruping welcome or the insistent demand (described in the next section). It is a series of fairly short but unhurried miaows, often interspersed with purring. As usual, the Siamese will use a lower-pitched note, with multiple inflections in which it is easy to distinguish pleasure, complaint, indignation, and so forth. The domestic cat uses a higher-pitched and more monotonous cry whose interpretation takes practice.

Although nobody can claim sufficient

knowledge of cat talk to be able to tell precisely from this information where the cat has been and what it has been doing, it is very easy to identify, for example, the Siamese way of telling you that he has been enjoying himself. The short miaows take on a definite inflection that sounds like "yak-yak-yak." This means "I have been having a happily adventurous time." The scope and excitement of the adventure can be gauged by the volume and duration of the "yak-yakking."

A cat who has been bored or frustrated or actively unhappy will let you know it by tingeing his short mews with a plaintive, minor note or, in extreme cases, with a distinct suggestion of a yowl. It should be realized that these inflections superimposed on the short, informatory miaow do not imply that the cat is *now* unhappy or bored. He is giving you his account of past events.

Once the talk session is over, it will very likely be suppertime; and if food is not forthcoming you will almost certainly be called upon for an explanation.

The Demand

Anybody who has ever owned a cat will recognize the demand. High-pitched, sustained, incessantly repeated, and absolutely infuriating. It reaches its zenith, of course, when a hungry cat is demanding food. But slightly watered-down versions of the same sound will tell you that the door is closed and your cat wishes to go out (or come in), that the state of the cat box is unsatisfactory and should be changed at once, that somebody has left a pile of books on his favorite chair, that he wishes to be lifted up to roost on some high and inaccessible shelf (this applies in particular to Siamese.)

The difficulty with the demand is not identifying it (anybody can do that) but putting a stop to it without complying with the terms laid down. A very firm "No!" (a word that must be taught from kittenhood) followed by an explanation ("It's too early," "It's cold outside—you wouldn't like it," or even a blunt "Because I say so!") will generally reduce the volume. Once again, the main thing is to react, to show the cat that you have heard and understood and will take action as soon as possible or at the appropriate time. A demanding cat who is ignored will redouble his imperatives until human beings lose patience and resort to obscenity or even violence, and as in the old nursery phrase, the whole thing inevitably ends in tears.

If your cat is justified in his demand, then omit the "No!"; do not raise your voice, but explain why you cannot comply with his request. I find that my cats, given a reasonable explanation (such as "I know it's past your suppertime, but I have to finish this letter to catch the mail. Then I'll feed you.") will shut up and wait with perfectly good-humored patience, continuing their demands only in concentrated, silent gazing from their enormous eyes. Again, if the cat behaves himself and stops his demands, reward him with praise. As with people, a little appreciation and flattery goes a long way. The next time, he will shut up more readily.

Sometimes mingled with the demand, but nevertheless distinct from it, is an aggrieved note.

The Complaint

Basically, the cry of complaint is the high-pitched demand, but it is laced with a plaintive, falling cadence. The "Mee-ow" comes out in two distinct syllables, with heartrending effect. Situations such as a dirty cat box produce an almost perfect blend of the demand and the complaint; whereas the complaint is entirely absent from demands for food. A pure complaint, unlaced with demand, is brought on by actual physical discomfort, such as cold, dampness, or getting shut in a broom closet.

Now, a cat who finds himself in a silly situation, almost certainly through his own stupidity or foolhardiness, and then sits there complaining about it often appears pretty comic to his human friends. And because complaining, whether in cats or people, is not an attractive characteristic, I see no harm in indulging in a little gentle mockery, so long, of course, as the cat is not in any serious discomfort or danger. The cat will not like it, because his dignity will be in question, but he may complain a little less in the future.

Quite different is the reaction of the cat who is really frightened or hurt. This is simply an expression of pure fear.

Panic

On some occasions, when the cat is taken by surprise, all dignity deserts him, and he emits a frantic squawk. If the danger is real or the hurt severe, the squawk is bloodchilling and must be taken seriously. Drop everything, and run to see what is the matter. However, cunning and pampered cats become adept at letting loose a panic signal in much less grave circumstances with the idea of attracting attention. Belinda is especially good at this. She has three panic yells: the genuine, which is a true scream of fright; the genuine but not serious, which she uses, for instance, when her tail is accidentally treaded on (a fairly frequent occurrence because she delights in twisting herself around the feet of people carrying laden trays or large parcels, especially when they are going up or down stairs); and finally, the mock panic, used when she has not actually been stepped on but thought that she might be. There is a halfhearted quality about this last cry that is unmistakable. Her objective in the last two cases is the same: to be picked up, made much of, and apologized to. The resultant purring is deafening.

There is another scream, but it is milder than the scream of panic.

The Protest

The protest is the exact equivalent of a child's whining, "I don't *want* to." It is a plaintive, high-to-low cadence, uttered without too much conviction, and much lower in pitch than the complaint. The cat knows very well that in the end, he will have to submit to taking the medicine, being brushed, or having his ears cleaned or his claws clipped. As a matter of form, however, the protest must be made. A cat who is already protesting needs very little provocation to slip into the mock-panic cry. Soothing, cheerful conversation, reassurance, and stroking are the best antidotes, together with a little banter. "Come on, now, you know it doesn't hurt. Don't be a crybaby."

Spot, whenever he visits the veterinarian, goes into a big protest-cum-mock-panic demonstration as soon as his box is opened in the doctor's office. Starting with a fairly mild protest, his miaows get louder and louder and turn into mock panic and finally genuine panic screams as the doctor attempts to lift him gently out onto the table. By the time he actually gets his inoculation, he is yelling so hard that he doesn't even notice the needle going in.

The people most affected by these histrionics are the owners of other animals, awaiting their turn with the doctor, who turn pale as Spot's screams effortlessly penetrate any soundproofing between the waiting room and the examining room. Many times I have emerged with Spot, quiet now and gazing smugly from his basket, to see white-faced people clutching their pets to their bosoms in alarm. Many times I have been asked, "Was the poor cat in terrible pain? What *did* the vet do to him?" My smiling reassurance that it was only a painless flu shot is often met with hostile stares of frank disbelief, and I am sure I am suspected of callous indifference to Spot's frightful agony.

Somewhere between the protest and the mild sort of panic comes another note.

Indignation

The chief characteristic of the indignant sound is self-righteousness. It is a single, high note uttered in short, sharp syllables and indicates that the cat has a legitimate grouse that he feels would stand up in a court of law (perhaps another cat has eaten his dinner, or the door separating him from his cat box has been inadvertently closed.) If the situation is not remedied promptly, indignation will soon turn to demand and probably complaint as well. Few cats can resist the temptation to rub it in when they feel put upon and completely in the right.

Many people find the exaggeratedly moral tone of the indignant call very amusing and tend to laugh at the cat who uses it. Try not to, even if it is funny. The very fact that your cat employs indignation shows that he has grasped the concept that he is legally entitled to certain things, which carries the corollary that he also knows that there are things to which he is *not* entitled. In fact, he has come quite a long way on the complicated psychological path towards the comprehension of an abstract conception: the awareness of right and wrong. So rather than mockery, he deserves congratulation, commiseration, and prompt restitution of his rights.

A cat who feels put upon might be expected to become short-tempered with his human companions, and indeed, cats have telling ways in which to make you aware of their displeasure. However, vocalized rage is seldom, if ever, directed at human beings, and then only if the cat is also very frightened. It is towards other animals, most frequently feline intruders or rivals, that he expresses that emotion.

Anger

The angry warning takes the form of a low-pitched growling at the outset, a curious sustained noise coming from the back of the throat, sounding like a mixture of a dog's growl and a very deep miaow. It is accompanied by a rhythmic lashing back and forth of the tail as the cat crouches and glares at the object of his fury. The other cat will probably reply in the same manner, and these exchanges can go on for a considerable time without either cat giving ground or advancing.

From the human point of view, it is good to be able to identify the sound and recognize it for what it is: the natural expression of an instinctive sense of territory and protection of the home from intruders. It very seldom erupts into actual violence but will become interspersed with hissing and spitting if the other cat attempts defiance.

Like the purr, angry noises appear to be triggered involuntarily. A friend of mine frequently used to bring her cats to visit us, and our cats would routinely growl and spit at them, although they never attacked them. However, if my friend came to our house alone, the cats would begin growling and spitting at her, obviously a reflex reaction set off by her association with alien cats and perhaps by their scent, which she carried. After a little while, their intelligence would reassert itself, they would realize that her cats were not with her, and they would greet her politely and a little sheepishly. It is interesting that cats who have developed the beginnings of a reasoning brain appear to be aware of the fact that instinct can be stronger than common sense, and they will struggle to suppress that instinct, as in the case of the cross cat who tries not to purr.

As a rule, confrontations over territory end mildly with the cat-in-possession victorious as the intruder beats a slow, cautious retreat, usually backward. Occasionally, however, the outsider will have the impertinence to advance. This may provoke a more intense response.

The Active Threat

Sound and action come together here with an impact that generally appears much more alarming than it really is. The home-based cat will move swiftly into the attack, with a lightning spring forward, a flash of flailing claws, and a bloodthirsty shriek. All this is largely a formal display and will probably have its desired effect of sending the other cat packing. It is a mistake to try to interfere in spats of this sort; you will only complicate matters and cause trouble. Cats, like most other animals, are perfectly capable of working out their differences in their own way and, unlike people, do not resort to violence against their own species except in a very few unusual cases. One of these, of course, involves the opposite sex.

Courtship

Tomcats will fight each other in the rough-and-tumble of back-alley courtship, although, as I have pointed out, in a protected cat colony, couples will form and live more or less monogamously in harmony with other couples. A neutered male who is allowed out at night may easily get mixed up in these brawls and come home with bites and lacerations. I don't imagine that it is necessary to describe the caterwauling that accompanies the fighting, but it is advisable to break things up if your cat is involved. I find that it is quite easy to distinguish the voices of my cats from those of the others, even if they are in full and hideous cry; and if I detect either of them, I take immediate action.

Outside lights on, doors and windows opened, and urgent calling are generally enough to scatter the combatants and bring our cats home at the gallop. If these methods fail, however, the best remedy is cold water, just as depicted on old-fashioned comic postcards. Cats hate getting wet, and although the water does them no harm, it effectively takes their minds off whatever they are doing, and that includes fighting. Never turn a strong jet from a hose on a cat; it is unnecessarily violent and can do harm. Just a sprinkle will do the trick. Then get your own cat back indoors by using his special call sign.

Personal Call

The personal call is at once the most interesting and the most difficult category to define, and that is because the precise sounds made by both cat and owner are entirely individual. In Chapter Three, I outlined how to lay the foundation for this invaluable system of communication, starting in kittenhood or at your first contact with the cat and using a food call in the early stages.

The first objective, not too difficult to attain, is to reach the point where you can be sure that the cat will come when he hears your particular call. It has been emphasized that he should always be rewarded by a small tidbit of food, even if it is not a regular mealtime, until his response to the call becomes so automatic that he will not even ask for food unless he is especially hungry. This stage should be reached after about a year.

The cat then recognizes your special call and will come to you in response to it. This is the first and most important step, but there remains the question of getting him to answer you. Some cats will do this automatically. A naturally talkative cat who comes running in the confident expectation of receiving food will certainly vocalize his pleasure and excitement; and if your call is consistent, his will be, too. Before long, the cat's call will become an automatic reply to your voice rather than the mere anticipation of food.

However, if your cat is more taciturn and does not evolve his own reply spontaneously, he can be encouraged to do so by the simple ruse of withholding his food from him until he asks for it. That is, when he arrives in response to your personal call, have the food plate in your hand and hold it above his head, talking encouragingly to him. He will probably stand on his hind legs, reaching up for the dish, but do not give it to him until he demands it vocally. With a little patience, this routine will produce a consistent cry from the cat that he will soon learn to produce as he approaches you in order to get the food more quickly. You will now have brought him, by a rather longer route, to the same point as your garrulous cat. From here on, the gradual phasing out of the food follows the same pattern with both types of cats.

When you have succeeded in eliminating the purely food-oriented response, be sure always to congratulate your cat when he answers your call, stroking him and making much of him, In this way, your love and encouragement will take the place of food as a reward for his response and will ensure that the two-way communication is always a pleasurable experience for the cat. Always remember that a cat's behavior depends on what pleases him, not on what he is forced to do. Not until he goes through the unpleasant experience of getting lost will he realize the practical advantages of his personal call sign. Meanwhile, he will cooperate with you for love and for the fun of it.

As a final appendage to this catalog of cat sounds, there is a nonsound that cats use with devastating effect. I refer, of course, to what Paul Gallico called "the silent miaow."

The Silent Miaow

The silent miaow is exactly what it sounds like: the mouth opens, the head goes back, all the gestures of mewing are there, but no sound emerges. Gallico related it mainly to the feline ploy of getting a human disciplinarian (often the man of the family) to break his own rules, such as No food from the dining table. The cat will station himself beside the man, fix him with an unblinking stare, and give him the silent miaow. This says several things: "I am *not* bothering anybody by demanding food from the table"; "You and I have a special relationship which *she* can never share"; "Since I was clever enough to make no noise, you can slip me a bit of your steak and she'll never know"; and "You must admit that I am a most appealing and clever little cat." This tactic has a very high success rate.

I have observed, however, that the silent miaow is used on other occasions as well, and the emphasis seems to be on the special relationship. For example, if Belinda (a great one for the silent miaow) wishes to have a door opened, she will demand it silently from my husband or myself but vocally from anybody else. Spot, at the end of a long and enjoyable talk session, will tone down his voice progressively until he is conversing silently. There is no doubt that there is something subtly flattering and delightful about being the human recipient of a silent miaow, as though a favorite person were whispering sweet nothings for your ears alone. Cats, of course, are well aware of this and exploit it to the full—that is, they use it sparingly enough to make sure that it will always be effective.

CHAPTER FIVE

BODY LANGUAGE

A cat's body is not only one of the most graceful and beautiful of natural things; it is also extremely eloquent. Only in the crisis situation of a fight, and in the intimacies of courtship and motherhood, do cats vocalize to each other. Their normal communication is by means of body language. Even the most untutored alley cat has a most sensitive and sophisticated range of messages, which he transmits largely by the precise use of tail and ears, although the whole body is brought into play to express some moods.

The Lick

The most direct and all-pervasive method of contact between cats of the same family or colony

is the lick, and this is extended to human beings who qualify for an intimate relationship. Some people are not overly fond of being licked by cats; I am one of them. But I put up with it, at least to a limited extent, because I realize that it is a great compliment and that to reject it would be interpreted as a personal rejection and withdrawal of love, which is the worst thing that can happen to a cat.

The lick is the most basic experience of a cat's life because the rasp of his mother's rough tongue is the first sensation a newborn kitten experiences. The mother cat extracts the kitten from the transparent, liquid-filled sac in which he is born and licks him vigorously to dry his coat and get him moving and to clear his mouth so that he can take his first breaths and make his first cries. From then on, his young life is filled with licking, for it is the way his mother grooms and cleans him. And she washes him from head to tail several times a day. It is obvious that the memory of these early weeks lingers on in adult cats, for they find licking the most natural way of expressing affection, and being licked the most comforting sensation in the world.

Among adult cats, licking fulfills the useful functions of mutual grooming and ear cleaning, but its symbolic significance goes much deeper. It is restricted to a small circle of intimates, both feline and human, and implies complete acceptance and trust. It is also an indicator of mood.

There is, for instance, the worried lick. If our two cats find themselves in a frightening or unsettling situation—shut up in their carrier in a crowded and noisy airport building, for example—they will go into a perfect frenzy of mutual licking, as if for reassurance. In the same way, they will lick my hand in a sort of desperate attempt to divert my purpose if they suspect (rightly) that they are about to be given pills or subjected to some other unpleasantness.

There is also the propitiatory lick, which, combined with a general body writhe, is an overt statement of a guilty conscience. This lick is administered with the ears well back and the eyes half closed and with the same urgency as the worried lick. It should not take you long to find the spilled milk or the broken vase for which your cat

is apologizing and from which he is trying to divert your attention.

More usual, however, is the affectionate lick, the highest accolade a cat can bestow on a person. It is reserved for moments of relaxation, contentment, and utter trust. Because, unlike the purr, the lick is an entirely voluntary expression of affection, the cat can and does withhold it in order to express dissatisfaction of one sort or another with his human friends. A cat who is in regular communication with his people often plays the no-lick ploy as a game, refusing all blandishments for a while and then relenting and administering a plethora of licks to the accompaniment of delighted purring.

Ears and Tail

The ears and tail, usually working in conjunction, can express a huge gamut of emotions. Sarah Bernhardt is reputed to have asked a surgeon if he could graft a leopard's tail onto her back; she felt unable to express herself adequately without one. I, for one, can see her point of view.

The first sign of anger in a cat is a rhythmic, horizontal lashing of the tail, quite gentle at first, but growing more and more pronounced if the animal is further provoked. This is accompanied by folding the ears flat, so that they lie parallel to the head instead of pointing upward. The exact angle of the ears and degree of energy in the tail convey precisely whether the cat is merely irritated and is giving fair warning of the fact or whether he is seriously annoyed and prepared to go into action if necessary.

If the cause of his anger is another animal, these signs will be accompanied by a fluffing up of the tail and coat. This is a natural and involuntary reaction designed to make the cat look larger and therefore more formidable to an enemy. In fact, any sudden noise, however innocuous its source, that catches the cat by surprise will provoke this stove-brush tail reaction. Belinda, in particular, always feels very foolish when her tail has automatically fluffed up for no better reason that

a dropped plate or a car backfiring, and she will proceed to lick it energetically to smooth down the ruffled fur. On the other hand, in the course of some of her more boisterous games, she will deliberately provoke the reaction by pretending to be scared, so I can only conclude that the fluffing process carries some element of pleasurable excitement with it.

A cat who is happily stimulated by the arrival of his owner or the anticipation of a meal will carry his tail very high and straight, like a banner. If he is disappointed, the tail will droop accordingly. In a more subtle way, both tail and ears are used to react when a cat knows that he is the subject of human conversation. He will sit or

crouch with his back to you, but at the mention of his name, the tip of the tail will twitch and one ear will quiver.

If the cat suspects that he is being mocked, the tail twitch becomes more pronounced, until it verges on an angry reaction. Cats are very sensitive to being laughed at, but fortunately they also have a sense of humor. A cat will take a joke at his expense in good part, so long as the perpetrator is one of his special people, someone with whom he has good communication going. A little verbal teasing will soon result in the swinging tail being replaced by a slightly reluctant grin.

The ears alone are a sure indication of various moods. In the jargon of our family, a slight sideways flattening of the ears is known as "putting on a hat." Hats are worn whenever a cat is suspicious or uncertain about anything: a strange noise, an

unfamiliar visitor, or an unknown hotel room. Sometimes the cause of suspicion is obvious, but at other times a cat will flatten his ears for no apparent reason. "Why are you wearing your hat, Spot?" is a question frequently heard around our house, and a little investigation will reveal the answer.

A cat who flattens his ears backward rather than sideways is bent on mischief. He will run away from you, his ears back and his buttocks swinging, dancing on the tips of his toes and with his tail at half-mast, most explicitly bent on some sort of naughtiness. The fact that cats will signal their intentions so obviously leads me to conclude that part of the fun is to attract human attention and invite pursuit.

Quite different, however, is the "please catch me" pose adopted during energetic chasing games. Cats are highly strung, nervous creatures, and although they get a thrill out of a mock chase (so long as the pursuer is a loved and trusted human) suddenly the game will get a little too authentic for comfort, and the cat will decide to put an end to it by abdicating. Abruptly, he ceases to run away and crouches down in the wild creatures' stance of surrender, tense but offering no resistance, like a rabbit mesmerized by a fox. I find this utter surrender both moving and distressing, and as I scoop the cat up into my arms (all purrs, now) I thank God that it is only a game.

Paws and Claws

Paws are used in direct-contact communication between cats and people, as well as between cats. A brisk slap with a front paw expresses anger or impatience and is also used in a disciplinary sense, undoubtedly a throwback to the mother cat's gentle nose taps by which she guides and corrects her kittens. Probably it is this instinctive memory that causes cats to aim their paw slaps at the face, whether of another cat or a human being. Another contributing factor is the defense mechanism of the cat, for when attacked by a larger and stronger animal, he lashes out with his claws at his opponent's most vulnerable spot, the eyes.

In this connection, I remember only too well when Belinda, a six-month-old kitten, was attacked in a Swiss meadow by a full-grown, cat-killing Doberman Pinscher bitch. Jim and I did what we could to protect Belinda, but we were quite powerless against the fantastic speed and strength of the dog. Belinda saved herself. She fought off the Doberman for the half minute or so that it took her to get to the foot of a tall tree, where, of course, she escaped by a lightning climb. I shall never forget the sight of that tiny kitten fighting off the snapping jaws of the huge dog. In fact, Belinda was not much longer than the Doberman's long-jawed head, and it was the head that she attacked.

The kitten was up on her hind legs, her tail was fluffed up to its fullest extent, a pathetically inadequate way of intimidating a killer dog! Her front paws, however, were doing the trick. Moving so fast that Muhammad Ali's fists could hardly have rivaled them, Belinda's paws with claws fully unsheathed flailed against the dog's nose, reaching for the eyes. To close her jaws on the kitten, the Doberman would have had to bring her eyes within reach of those claws, and this she was not prepared to do. Nature has equipped the cat with an extremely efficient weapon and the instinct to use it to its fullest extent.

The fact that a cat's claws are capable of inflicting serious physical damage is one of the reasons that some people are afraid of cats. Please don't be. The cat's claws are used for hunting small creatures and for defense against large ones. Against people, they are used only in defense; and my view is that if a human being attacks a cat, I hope he does get his eyes scratched out.

A cat who wishes to express displeasure with his paws will first administer a gentle, admonitory tap, with claws fully sheathed. In the case of my own cats, Spot will never go further than this. He may tap a little harder, but he has never wittingly scratched a human being. Belinda, on the other hand, has evolved a system of her own that we have come to know well. Let us say that you have picked her up, and she wishes to be put down again. The first sign of her displeasure is a gentle, clawless tap on the cheek. If this is ignored, she gives you another tap, less gentle. After these two warnings, she will flatten her ears and tap again, but this time just a fraction of claw is protruding, enough to ensure that her instructions are obeyed. Needless to say, she would never give a person a serious scratch, but she is a lady who likes to have her own way and who knows how to get it.

On the other hand, paws are also used to express love and affection. A cat greeting a human friend will often stand on his hind legs and reach up with his front paws to stroke and caress his friend's hands. This is frequently accompanied by a butting of the top of the cat's head against the person's legs, loud purring, and possibly the welcoming call as well. Cats will also embrace a human leg or arm with their front paws, generally as a plea to the person not to leave them.

Another very endearing habit is the gentle, deliberate placing of a velvet-soft paw on the nose of a person who is holding the cat in his arms. A friend of ours, utterly captivated by his first Siamese kitten, used to demonstrate this affectionate gesture to his friends with immense pride, claiming (correctly) that the kitten did it quite spontaneously and with no teaching and (incorrectly) that his kitten was undoubtedly the only one in the world who was sweet enough to caress her master's nose. Nobody was unkind enough to break it to him that nearly all cats do it once their love and trust have been gained.

In fact, cats love to use their paws to caress their special people, expecially about the face. I saw a remarkable instance of this when Belinda was quite a young cat. As I have indicated, Jim is her special person; and when he has to go away from home, she grows very depressed and obviously misses him a lot. One evening, while Jim was away at a Conference in Africa, Belinda and Spot and I were all watching television when on the screen came a big close-up of a man who looked remarkably like my husband.

Belinda had been paying little attention to the television set until then, but suddenly she sat up, her ears pricked and alert. Then she jumped off the sofa, ran to the screen, and stood up on her hind legs, caressing the man's face with her front paws. Then the picture changed abruptly, and she dropped back onto all fours and came dejectedly back to me, losing all interest in the set. She had never done such a thing before, nor has she since. It may sound farfetched, but I can only believe that she really imagined that Jim was somehow inside the television set. She certainly appeared to recognize the face, and the resemblance *was* most striking. When we first acquired a television set, both cats used to react to the appearance of other cats on the screen, but they soon realized that the whole thing was an illusion and not worth bothering about. The sole exception was the incident I have just recounted.

While on the subject of paws, I want to register a strong protest against the practice of declawing cats, which is quite rare in Europe but is becoming all too prevalent in the United States. The idea, of course, is to preserve valuable furniture and rugs from damage, and owners swear that, if performed under anesthetic by a good surgeon, the procedure is painless and does not inconvenience the cat. This is ridiculous. Quite apart from the fact that recovery is always painful, the enormity of the offense is that it deprives the cat of his only means of defense.

Not only are the claws a cat's natural weapon, but without them he cannot climb; and if he cannot climb, he is helpless against his enemies. This means that a declawed cat can never, under any circumstances, be allowed to go out of doors; and even in his own home, he must constantly be protected against visiting animals. A cat living this sort of half life is truly emasculated, to a far

greater extent than his neutered or spayed brothers and sisters. He can exist only in the pampered,
overheated world of his owners. He can never
climb a tree or play in long grass or walk in the
woods or even sleep safely in the sun in his own
backyard. I beg anybody who thinks more of his
furniture than of his cat not to acquire a pet of
any sort.

Whiskers

Whiskers have a special vocabulary all their
own. Nature provides them as a sort of sixth sense
for cats in tight places. A cat's whiskers are extremely sensitive, and although they may not actually provide a gauge of the cat's body width, as
popular superstition has it, they do guide him in
dark and confined spaces. Incidentally, it is not
true that cats can see in total darkness, but they
can see better than most mammals in dim light,
and their whiskers help them by adding tactile
perception to vision.

However, when not fulfilling this useful func-
tion, the whiskers are an eloquent barometer of
feelings and emotions. A curious, investigative cat
will extend his whiskers to their full span,
twitching with excitement; a bored, listless cat
will allow his whiskers to droop; a restful, contented cat will lay his whiskers flat against his muzzle,
extending from mouth to ear, often accompanied

by a broad smile, which makes the cat look almost comically complacent.

The Smile

This brings me to the question of whether or not cats can smile. I have heard it asserted by some authorities that they cannot, and I can only presume that these people have never owned a cat in the true sense of the word. As with dogs, the smile has nothing to do with baring the teeth (some dogs are taught to draw back their lips in a savage parody of a grin, which their owners proudly describe as smiling). The real smile, in cats or dogs, is a relaxed upward tilting of the corners of the mouth, and it is instantly recognizable. Cats often smile in their sleep, sometimes when they are obviously having happy dreams, as revealed by whisker twitching and paw kneading; at other times, if gently stroked while asleep, they do not wake up but smile broadly.

Eyes

A cat's eyes are every bit as expressive as a human being's, in fact, rather more so because they are more versatile. As everyone knows, the iris of a cat's eye reacts almost instantaneously to variations in the intensity of light, opening up to give maximum exposure of the pupil in a dim light, and narrowing to a slit in bright light. Also, the cat has a third eyelid, a grayish membrane that comes up from the bottom of the eye. Normally, this membrane is not seen; it is completely retracted when the eye is open. However, if a cat is sick, the third eyelid may remain partially up and visible, and this is a danger signal to look out for.

Apart from these involuntary changes in the eyes, cats have a most attractive way of squeezing up their eyes to an almost-closed position when they are especially happy and relaxed. A cat who is lying comfortably, being stroked and spoken to, will keep his eyes in this half-closed manner while smiling and purring. However, it is even more endearing when your cat seeks you out in order to talk to you and accompanies his remarks, whether vocal or in body language, with a series of eye squeezes. While doing this, he never takes his intent gaze from your face, emphasizing his love and trust with eye movements. The eye squeeze in conjunction with the silent miaow is an irresistible combination.

Cats are especially good at the game of trying to outstare people, and it takes considerable strength of mind not to blink or be the first to look away when faced by those huge, unwavering eyes of green, blue, or gold.

CHAPTER SIX

TALKING TO YOUR CAT

It seems presumptuous to try to dictate to any-body how to respond to his or her own pet, but for people who have not perhaps realized the full potential of communication between cat and hu-man being, a few pointers may be helpful.

The first and most important rule is to talk to your cat easily, freely, and without self-conscious-ness. Overestimate his intelligence, treat him as a reasonable being, and he will soon start behaving like one. By the same token, as his personality de-velops under the stimulus of human contact, he will become more self-willed and generally smart-er. This means that you must at all costs avoid sentimentality, slack discipline, constant between-meal snacks, and other indulgences, for he will quickly learn to twist you around his paws if you are not very careful.

Before we go any further, let us make sure that we understand what I mean by discipline. I do not mean anything harsh and most certainly not corporal punishment. A sharp "No!", a firm and disapproving tone of voice, a momentary withdrawal of affection, and a gentle tap on the nose are all that are needed. The most important thing is to make the rules early on and then stick to them. In my experience, people who make a great fuss about discipline are usually the first to breach it for their own amusement; then they overreact with anger and a certain amount of guilt when the cat assumes that the rule has been suspended and breaks it again.

Discipline need not be unpleasant or overemphasized. A properly brought up kitten will learn the rules so easily and at such a tender age that he will regard them as part of life and not at all irksome. For instance, there is the vexed question of food scraps from the dining table.

Now, there is nothing more annoying, unhygienic, or calculated to create animal haters than pets who beg for food during meals. Their owners may possibly regard the practice as cute or may have got so used to it that they hardly notice it anymore, but it is an abuse to expect guests to put up with it. On the other hand, cats adore small pieces of salmon, turkey, roast beef, and other delicacies, and these excellent foods do them no harm and give them an enormous amount of pleasure. If permissiveness is bad, overrigid authoritarianism is worse. So what is the answer?

It is very simple. Give the cats their tidbits, but after the meal and in the kitchen. If a cat has never *ever* been fed anywhere except in the kitchen, that is the only room in the house that he associates with food. Also, if he knows that he will eventually get his share of the family treat, he will not feel obliged to beg or badger. When we have a particularly delicious meal, the cats will station themselves in the kitchen before it is over, waiting eagerly for the small treat that they know they will get. They do not even consider the idea of getting food in the dining room, because in their minds it is simply not a place where cats eat; they do not feel deprived or disciplined by that fact. It's just the way things are.

Scratching furniture is a more difficult matter. By allowing cats access to trees (their natural scratching posts), or by providing plenty of scratchers indoors, or both, you can make sure that your cat has no *need* to scrape off the dead outer nails on your furniture. On the other hand, cats quickly realize that this forbidden activity is a surefire attention-getter and will use it quite unscrupulously. The best advice I can give is that a happy cat who receives plenty of human contact and communication is the least likely to vent his frustration on a valuable sofa. But you never can be quite sure.

Listening is as important as talking when communicating with your cat. We all know the irritation and boredom generated by the person who rattles on and on and never pauses to hear *your* point of view. Remember that your cat feels the same way, so let him talk, encourage him, question him, answer him, sympathize with him, but above all, listen.

All this requires a commodity that is precious to many people: time. Few of us can afford the luxury of sitting down and devoting half an hour or so of our day just to talk to cats, although, come to think of it, many half hours are spent less profitably. However, most people can snatch a few minutes, especially in the evening, to devote to their pets. The main thing is to let the cats know that you are responding, that you can hear them.

In the early stages of cat-person dialogue, progress is best achieved by reacting in harmony with the cat, that is, being happy when he is happy and sad when he is sad. However, as with all meaningful exchanges between living creatures, a far deeper understanding will grow up until eventually you can respond to his joyful evening greeting with, "Well, I'm glad you had a good day because mine was lousy and I'd like a little sympathy." The beautiful thing is that you will get it. You must, of course, be prepared to do the same for your cat should the circumstances be reversed.

Once you have started talking to your own cat,

you will very soon find that you can pick up the dialect, as it were, and converse with all sorts of strange cats. Personally, I can never pass a cat in the street without greeting it and exchanging a few words, and the cat invariably replies.

There is a charming story told about the great French writer Colette, who was totally in sympathy with cats. She was never very happy in the United States, she spoke little or no English, and she felt out of sympathy with the hustle and bustle of New York City. One evening, making her way back to her hotel after a brash Manhattan party, she spotted a small black cat sitting on a wall and of course went over to speak to it. After a satisfactory exchange of pourparlers, Colette turned to her human companion with a brilliant smile. *"Enfin!"* she said. *"Quelqu'un qui parle Français!"* ("At last! Somebody who speaks French!")

And there you have it. The Bible tells us that human beings were punished for their hubris at the Tower of Babel by being divided into a multilingual society, losing direct vocal contact with each other. Ever since, people have been trying to evolve a universal language. Latin was the most successful, lasting for many hundreds of years as the means of communication between the educated people of Europe. In the end, however, the movement towards the vernacular was too strong, and even dog Latin disappeared as a common tongue.

French made a gallant effort, establishing itself as the language of diplomacy for a couple of centuries, but it is clearly doomed. English, the latest champion in the field, is beginning to suffer from the pressures of national pride and a desire to dig down to ethnic roots. Esperanto was one of those splendid ideas that never really got off the ground. And all the time, very quietly, cats have been speaking to us in a language that any human being can understand so long as he loves his cat. There must be a moral there, somewhere.

Cats love secrets. They delight in finding secret places in the house to hide and sleep, they like to disappear on secret errands out of doors, and they adore being told secrets, which is to say, they love it if you whisper to them. What you whisper may be nonsense, but that does not matter; the cat will react with the utmost pleasure and will in return honor you with his confidences. This is a very intimate process and will bring you close to your cat and make future communication progressively easier.

Play is a basic form of communication, and here again it is important to let the cat decide on the games. Present him with alternatives based on the simplest of toys, and then observe his reactions. I find that a small, rolled-up ball of tinfoil is universally appreciated by cats. It is light, it makes an intriguing noise when skittering over floors, it is versatile, and it stimulates the imagination.

Here are a few of the tinfoil games that various

cats have taught me. There is the fetch-and-carry game, in which the person throws the paper ball and the cat retrieves it, carries it carefully back in his mouth, and drops it at the person's feet. Belinda has her own variation on this game. She likes me to take one shoe off, and then she very precisely drops the paper ball into the empty shoe. This was entirely her own idea.

Then there is the hide-and-seek game. In this, the tinfoil ball is concealed by the person and found by the cat. Once again, this was Belinda's invention, and she very soon cottoned to the idea of going out of the room while I was hiding the ball. She would find one of the many balls that she always keeps hidden around the house, bring it to me, and drop it at my feet. If she then waited expectantly, I knew that she wanted to play fetch-and-carry; but if she immediately ran out of the room on tiptoe, her tail arched and her ears back in the naughty-expectant-excited position, I knew it was to be hide-and-seek. I would then conceal the ball under a cushion or behind a book and give Belinda's special call. She would come dancing in and eagerly begin exploring the hiding places.

As a young cat, she became expert at this game, and by her looks of disgust if the paper was too easy to find, she egged me on to find more and more difficult hiding places. I talk of this game in the past tense because for some reason she aban-

doned it altogether after the birth of her kittens. I suppose she felt it beneath the dignity of a cat who had taken on the responsibilities of motherhood.

A game which she still plays, however, is the carry-down game. For this, the tinfoil ball is balanced on some high place, such as the top of a chair back, the handle of a chest of drawers, or a stair banister. The important thing is that the cat must be obliged to stand on his hind legs to reach the ball. The game is to dislodge the ball, using front paws and teeth, and to carry it to the ground without dropping it. Belinda, with her delicacy and great sense of balance, is very good at it. Spot, whose best friend could not describe him as delicate, has never really grasped the concept of this game. He simply rushes for the ball, dislodges it so that it falls to the ground, and turns to me with a grin of triumph. When he does so, Belinda gives him a look of patronizing disgust, which has reduced strong men to helpless paroxysms of mirth. She will then indicate to me, by the merest squeak, that she wishes to give a demonstration. I replace the paper, and she proceeds to carry it down with a flourish and a lithe grace, to applause from one and all. She drops it at my feet (or in my shoe), nods briefly to her audience, and departs. "*That*," she is saying, "is how *that* game should be played."

Another cat I know, Tito, a handsome black-and-white fellow, taught me a new tinfoil game when I was looking after him while his owners were away. I was throwing a tinfoil ball for him to chase, but he was obviously bored. I tried him on my own cats' games, but he showed little interest. Instead, when I produced the ball, he would stand on his hind legs and clap his front paws together in the air. Well, I may not be very bright, but I could interpret a simple message like that. Tito wanted a high-thrown ball that he could catch in his paws. He turned out to be an Olympic-class catcher. Not once did the ball escape those front paws, and he purred his appreciation of the fact that I had understood his request and acted upon it.

This is an illustration of what I mean by listening to your cat. Tito used most explicit body language to communicate with me. He was not a very vocal cat, but interestingly enough, he became more so during the weeks when I was visiting him twice a day. Of course, he lived with a loving, communicative family and was wide open to friendly overtures from his cat-sitter; but I was still impressed by the fact that within a week, we had developed an individual welcoming call. If he was upstairs or at the back of the house when I arrived, I would call him and hear his distinctive cry answering me as he came running to greet me.

Occasionally, play can get rough. Male cats, even if neutered, have a deeply ingrained instinct to bite and kick at the beloved object, and this object can be a human hand. If this happens to you, do not try to pull your hand away, or you may get hurt. On the contrary, relax your hand and talk gently to the cat. In a few seconds, he will give you an apologetic lick, let go of your hand, and retreat in considerable embarrassment. Do please understand that the apparent attack is never more than love biting and will do you no harm unless you try to snatch your hand away. If you do, it is you who will be the instigator of violence, not the cat.

To sum up, then, there are a few basic rules that should govern your response to your cat. The first is to respond generously, volubly, and unselfconsciously. The second is to listen as well as to talk. The third is to make regulations and keep to them rigidly, but without harshness. The fourth, and most important, is simply to love your cat.

Then, just by doing what comes naturally, you will very soon have a two-way communication system going that will enrich your life, delight your cat, and incidentally, make living with cats a simple and immensely enjoyable affair.

CHAPTER SEVEN

MINOR CRISES

Let me say right away that this is *not* a chapter devoted to cat's ailments and how to deal with them. My only advice on that subject is that if your cat appears to be ill, take him to a veterinarian right away. Amateur diagnosis and treatment will probably do no good and may do harm; so may delay in getting your pet to his doctor. Your cat will tell you in many ways if he is not well. You will notice loss of appetite, lassitude, a hot nose, a staring coat (one that is not sleek, but with the hairs standing vertically), and a marked lessening of vocal communication. If these symptoms persist, don't hesitate—take him to the doctor's office.

On the other hand, crises do occur in any life, and there will be times when you have to help your cat through such moments. Here are a few of the most frequently encountered.

Giving Birth

I do not regard giving birth to kittens as an illness. Naturally, if anything goes wrong, you should consult the veterinarian at once; but normally, a mother cat can cope very well on her own with a little assistance from you.

As soon as you know or suspect that your cat is pregnant, take her to the doctor for a checkup. I am assuming now that the kittens are wanted and are either purebred animals that can be sold or kittens that you intend to keep yourself or give to friends who want them. If the kittens are not deliberately planned for, then it is better and kinder to have your female cat aborted and spayed as early as possible in pregnancy. The operation is not serious; the cat soon recovers all her former zest for life; and although it is sad for both of you to be deprived of the joy and fun of having kittens, there is a great deal in the old saying that what you have never had, you don't miss.

However, we are talking about a planned family. The vet will tell you what supplements should be added to your cat's diet, and you should follow his instructions meticulously because correct feeding can make all the difference to the health of both the kittens and the mother. If your cat has been mated deliberately, you can calculate the estimated birth date; the gestation period is sixty-three days. Otherwise, the vet will give you his best guess on when to expect the birth.

Near the end of pregnancy, most cats will begin making a nest, usually in some highly unsuitable place such as the linen closet or the drawer in which you keep your most delicate clothes. This practice should be discouraged, but many cats are so cunning that you never find the nest until it is too late. However, if you take pains to construct a nest for your cat and explain to her exactly what you are doing, she will grasp the idea and very probably go along with it.

When Belinda was a few days away from the estimated birth date, I made a nest for her. She had not started to make a nest for herself, and she watched with interest as I went about the job and explained to her what I was doing. I used an empty wooden wine crate. Any sort of box will do, but wood is preferable to cardboard. The box must be large enough to allow the cat to lie down comfortably, fully extended. I then chose a quiet and secluded spot in the house, in a cool place because the birth was in July. In the winter, of course, you would pick somewhere warm. I arranged the box with its open side upward and then cut one of the long vertical sides down so that it was about six inches from the floor. This would enable Belinda to jump in and out easily but would prevent the kittens from escaping until they were old enough to look after themselves.

I lined the box with a lot of old newspaper, laid flat. It is comfortable, warm, smooth, and easily disposed of when soiled; blankets will only get ruined and are not really suitable anyway. Finally, I draped a piece of fairly dense, dark cloth loosely over the open top of the box. This was to allow plenty of air to get in while shading the kittens from too much light. It is especially important to keep them in semidarkness for the first few days after their eyes have opened.

Despite her interest, I found it hard to believe that Belinda really understood what I was doing, but obviously she did. She made no attempt to nest for herself, but on the appointed day, when she felt the birth pains coming on, she ran straight to the box, with no prompting from me, and stretched herself out in it, lying on her side.

Naturally, by this time I had equipped myself

with a small library of technical books on what to do if something goes wrong. Normally, all is well. But in view of Spot's somewhat erratic birth (as described in Chapter One), it was fortunate that I had taken the advice of the experts and equipped myself with some warm, rough towels, absorbent cotton, and warm water. I would advise you to do the same.

Kittens are generally born about half an hour apart, and the average litter is from four to six, although single births are quite frequent. Once again, if anything seems to be taking too long or causing too much distress, you should call the doctor.

Once all the kittens have been born, change the soiled newspapers and give the mother a drink of warm milk. So long as you have good communication with her, she will not mind at all if you handle the kittens and lift them out of the nest while the bedding is being changed. At this stage, though, it is best not to allow any visitors other than known and trusted members of the family. Strangers, however well-meaning, can make the new mother very nervous. After a few days, you may bring friends to see the kittens, but please do not let anyone other than yourself handle them until they are several weeks old, fully sighted and very much up and about.

Even the most rational, intelligent female cat resorts to pure instinct at such times—as do many rational, intelligent female humans—and any real or imagined threat to her family will cause her to behave almost hysterically, carrying the kittens by the scruffs of their necks away from the nest and to new hiding places and refusing to believe your assurances that no harm will come to them.

One of the miracles of cathood is that no kitten ever has to be housebroken. While the kittens are ingesting nothing but their mother's milk, she will lick them spotlessly clean several times a day, so that the nest is never dirty. However, once they begin to eat other food, which should be at around three weeks of age, you must provide a small cat box near the nest. It should be low enough for the kittens to climb into (they will be very active by then, jumping and tumbling over the cut-down side of the nest and exploring every nook and cranny of the room until checked by the soft tap of their mother's paw on their noses.)

Now, the authorities tell you that the mother cat teaches the kittens to use the cat box. Maybe. But let me tell you an absolutely true, cross-my-heart story.

It is quite difficult to persuade kittens to make the change from mother's milk and on to prepared baby food, which is what is recommended. Once a day, I provided a saucer of it, together with a small cat box. Belinda's kittens sat in the food, batted it at each other with their paws, and did everything but eat it. Every day the baby food had to be thrown away, and the cat box remained unused.

Belinda chose these times to leave her family with me and go downstairs to have a meal and use her own, adult-size cat box, so there was nobody present except me and the kittens on the day when the largest and firstborn (nicknamed Charlie) suddenly caught on. He lowered his chin into the milky fluid and began to lap it up. Then, after taking a good feed, he toddled fatly off, not towards the nest, but towards the cat box. He climbed laboriously into it, scraped a little hole in the litter, squatted down, and urinated.

I could not believe my eyes. Belinda was not even in the room at the time, so how could she have taught him, as the cat books claimed? Perhaps that beautiful chirruping call that the mother cat makes to her little ones conveys more precise information than we realize.

Kittens are ready to leave their mother at ten to twelve weeks. Both mother and offspring seem to sense this, and there is no great trauma at parting, so long as the kittens have been allowed to choose their own people (as described in Chapter Two). Do please check out the homes that your kittens are going to, and try to make sure that they, like their mother, will be in communication with their human families. The most important thing to say to a new owner is, "If there's trouble of any sort, please bring him back."

I can assure you that if the kitten is old enough to leave his mother, if he has chosen his own person, and if you have reassured yourself that he is going to a loving and communicative environment, the only tears shed will be your own. It is horrible parting with kittens.

Loss of Companion or Mate

However good communication with your cat may be, it is impossible to explain away the sudden disappearance of a feline companion, whether this is caused by death, stealing, or simply getting lost. Death following an illness or operation is the easiest to cope with because cats in the same human family nearly always respond to each other's illness, often keeping vigil at the sickbed of another cat as faithfully and patiently as they would at their owner's; so if the sick cat does die, the shock is not so great. However, if a companion cat simply disappears, the remaining cat will show signs of considerable shock and distress.

For a start, the survivor will become fanatically attached to his human owner and follow him everywhere. The very fact of a closed door between you and your pet will send him into a sort of hysteria of pitiful mewing. Obviously, it is very important to keep him with you as much as you can, talk to him, and make much of him. He will sense the acute distress that you are feeling at the loss of the other cat, and the two of you will have to try to console each other. Talk sessions should be frequent and prolonged; they will bring comfort to both parties.

A strange phenomenon that I have noticed in each of my cats when the other has been absent long enough to cause anxiety is mimicry. The two cats have completely different voices, and normally there is no mistaking which of them is talking. But under the strain of a temporary loss, when the whole family is searching and calling for the missing cat, the other will mimic the lost one's voice so accurately that I have been tricked into imagining that the wanderer has returned. I can only think that this arises from an obscure feeling that the sound of the longed-for voice will somehow bring comfort to the human friend.

Another phenomenon, less strange, is that when the strayed cat finally turns up, the home-based cat at first appears not at all pleased to see him back. He or she may even spit at or box the ears of the returned wanderer. It will probably be about twenty-four hours before the second cat is finally welcomed home with a plethora of licking. There are two possible explanations for this, both of which may be true to some extent.

First, the cat may be having exactly the same reaction as that of a distracted mother who, having pulled her child from under the wheels of a speeding car, proceeds to spank him soundly instead of hugging him. This, of course, is partly to warn him not to be so foolhardy again and partly to vent her subconscious anger against him for having subjected her to such intense anxiety.

Second, it may also be true that the stay-at-home cat has been enjoying all the love and attention lavished on him and that, despite his relief at seeing his companion come back, he is vaguely resenting the fact that maximum attention is now inevitably being given to the other cat. It is, in fact, precisely the reaction of the prodigal son's brother in the Bible story.

Suppose, however, that your second cat is not just missing but dead. The most important thing is to replace him as soon as possible, not with another adult cat, but with a kitten. It is very unlikely that the remaining cat will attack a small kitten, but just to be on the safe side, keep the two apart for a couple of days, until the kitten has settled in. Then introduce them to each other gradually.

The important thing is to avoid putting your cat's nose out of joint by making too much fuss over the small newcomer, however enchanting that little one may be. Let your cat realize that you love him as much as ever and that he is now undisputedly Senior Cat. Most cats are fairly bossy by nature, and he will enjoy the feeling of superiority.

So make much of both cat and kitten. Flatter the adult cat. And, as far as possible, do not interfere. Let them work out the situation themselves. Within a very short time, they will be the best of friends.

Cats in Trees

The cat is not equipped by nature to engage in more than a rearguard action when attacked by a larger animal. That, of course, he achieves by going for his adversary's eyes with his claws, but this strategy cannot be kept up for very long. His ultimate method of self-preservation is climbing.

Unfortunately, when a cat has had a narrow brush with, say, a large and fierce dog and has finally reached the sanctuary of a tree, he is apt to lose his head and climb far higher than is necessary to ensure his escape. It is very much easier for him to go upward than it is for him to come down again. Consequently, you get the problem of the treed cat.

As an owner, it is very difficult to accept calmly the basic truth that if he got up there, he can get down again. Firemen with extending ladders are summoned, agile local children are encouraged to climb the tree, and nearly always the result is to drive the frightened cat even higher. When he is finally cornered, he will fight back in panic and may inflict quite serious damage on his rescuer.

In nearly every case, the best thing to do is to keep an eye on him (binoculars are a good idea) and wait until he feels secure enough to come down on his own. Of course, this is a situation where vocal communications is vital. Nothing will calm him down more quickly than the reassuring sound of his owner's voice giving his personal call sign and telling him that all's clear and he can safely descend.

When Belinda was a mere six months old and attacked by a large dog, she streaked up to the topmost branches of an enormously tall pine tree, a good sixty feet above ground. We were desperately worried about her. She was so young and tiny and had had absolutely no experience in serious tree climbing. At most, all she had ever done was to scoot about six feet up a small sapling and then come down by the simple method of sticking her head downward and falling to the ground. I was certain that she had not grasped the principle of climbing down backward in order to retain control with her claws. I had visions of her falling sixty feet and braking her neck.

We called and cajoled, but she refused to budge. She stayed in that tree for three hours, until she was completely satisfied that the menace had departed. Then, as I was about to have hysterics, she came down—very slowly and carefully, backward, like an expert. Ever since then, I have been convinced that a cat can and will come down in his own good time, however desperate the situation may appear, so long as he is not frightened by strangers. But, as I said, it is very difficult to convince yourself of this if it is your pet who is apparently marooned at a dizzy height.

Hunting

Cats are natural hunters, and it is no use reproaching them for it. After all, over the centuries men have encouraged them to kill rats and mice, and it is asking too much to expect them to differentiate between the domestic-mouse hunt, which is praiseworthy, and the field-mouse or bird hunt, which suddenly becomes a crime. Your cat will get confused or even neurotic if you try to meddle with his natural instincts.

In these circumstances, it is inevitable that cats will take pride in their hunting prowess and will

bring back grisly trophies for your inspection. One quartet of country-living cats I know arranges the night's kill in a neat row outside their owner's bedroom door early each morning and sits there purring, waiting for congratulations.

I am afraid that there is nothing to be done except to dispose of the pathetic little corpses. You need not actually praise the cat, but do not scold him either. It is not his fault that he is part and parcel of one of nature's less likable aspects, and after all, you are probably having beef or chicken for dinner yourself. Somebody had to kill it to get it to your table. And although you can, if your principles demand it, lead a healthy life as a vegetarian, your cat cannot.

Of course, if your cat brings home a mouse or a bird alive and uninjured, you can take it away from him and let it go. He may make a great show of being angry, but the betting is that if he has not killed it outright, he is not really interested in it and is glad to be disencumbered of it. Spot nearly always brings me the few small creatures that he catches, quite unharmed. He puts up a fearsome growling but no real resistance when I prise open his jaws and let his prey escape. Only on the rare occasions when Spot is hungry and hunts for food does he kill and eat his victim.

As an example of the ingenuity of cats, I give high place to the hunting habits of a cat named Nini, a female tabby found abandoned as a kitten, who belonged to my mother and who lived to be over twenty years old.

Nini's home was a large house in the country with a big garden in which she hunted nocturnally during the warm summer months. When autumn came, however, she would carefully bring her mice in alive and release them in the kitchen area, where she knew they would get enough to eat and would breed and multiply. She thus made sure that she would have game to hunt inside the house during the winter.

I have often seen her release a mouse in the larder and sit by complacently as he started in on the cheese. Whenever we caught her at it, two family members would go into action, one with a wastepaper basket and the other with a phonograph record. The job of the first was to drop the basket upside down over the mouse; the second would then slide the record under it, and thus captured, the mouse was returned to the garden, much to the disgust of the watching Nini.

However, she was usually too smart for us, and the result was that we regularly had a plague of mice in the house around October. Their numbers would begin to diminish during the cold November nights and would decrease steadily until, by the time April came with its balmy weather, there would not be a single one left.

Incidentally, this cat had fantastic communication going with my mother but cared not a jot for anybody else. If my mother had to go away for a few days, the cat would stalk out into the garden and stay there (provided the weather was not too cold), reappearing only briefly to take her food at the kitchen door. However, whether my mother was gone for two days or ten, on the day when she was expected home, Nini would mysteriously reappear in the house and would sit with her nose glued to a window overlooking the front door, waiting expectantly for her special person to come home.

Many skeptical visitors saw this happening and tried to explain it away, but none of the explanations held water. Some people believed that my mother must have established some sort of routine in her absences, going away for set periods at set intervals, but this was not so. Her trips were completely random. Others maintained that the cat must sense the general air of expectancy in the house on the day of the return, but, as I have

pointed out, she remained outside and away from the house until the actual day then came straight in and stationed herself at the window, even before being fed. The truth, which few people could bring themselves to accept, was simply that my mother always told Nini how many days she would be away and when she would be coming back.

I have left until last a minor crisis that can easily turn into a major one: the phenomenon of straying. In fact, this is a subject important and complex enough to deserve its own chapter.

CHAPTER EIGHT

STRAYING

I have laid such stress on the cat's qualities of loyalty, fidelity, and personal attachment to people that it may seem curious that I am now going to write about straying, that is, disappearances from home, sometimes voluntary, by loved, intelligent, and communicating cats. Nevertheless, this sometimes happens, and you should be prepared to understand the phenomenon.

A well-treated cat will leave home for two reasons. The first is curiosity, and the second is pique.

Everybody knows the old saying that curiosity killed the cat, and it is as true as ever. Cats simply cannot resist sticking their noses into everything, whether or not it is their business, and this habit gets them into all kinds of trouble. Sometimes the

109

outcome is tragic. The cat that dashes across the street to investigate a piece of fluttering wastepaper may end up under the wheels of a car; the cat that is determined to explore every corner of a dark shed may get locked inadvertently inside when the owners leave for a protracted holiday.

Incidentally, I heard a happy-ending story of an Anglo-Portuguese cat, living in Portugal, who got locked up in a neighbor's garage the day before his owners had to leave for England. Because they had no personal call-and-answer sign, they were unable to locate him and had to fly off without finding him. Three weeks later they returned. Still no cat. The next day, their neighbors came home and unlocked the garage, unaware that they had been harboring a lodger. The cat's owners were down at the beach and returned home to find their pet on the doorstep. He had dragged himself back to the house and, weakened after three weeks without food or water, collapsed. He was nursed back to health and, at the last report, was no worse for his adventure, which shows that cats are remarkably resilient and capable of survival under very harsh conditions.

The cat who leaves home because he is motivated by curiosity and who has established a two-way working call sign with his owner is comparatively easy to find. When we lived in our first rented house in Washington, Spot would frequently fail to turn up for his evening meal and

would be located, after a lot of personal call sign-
ing, shut up in a neighboring garage or toolshed.

The cat who leaves home out of pique is con-
siderably more difficult, if not impossible, to find;
but he will return home of his own free will once
he judges that you have been taught your lesson.
In my experience, cats who are out to demonstrate
disapproval will usually disappear in the evening,
stay out all night and the following day, and return during the subsequent night, always providing (and this is important) that access to the house
is available to them. If you do not live in a cli-
mate or locality in which you can leave doors and
windows open, I would strongly recommend a cat
door set into a door or window a few inches above
floor level that will allow your pet to come and go
as he wishes.

It is difficult to define just what human behavior drives a cat to the point of disappearance. It
can be as serious a pretext as his owner's prolonged absence (certainly the original reason why
Spot ran away in Washington, although he managed to get himself lost and isolated, and his absence soon ceased to be voluntary) or as frivolous a
reason as being teased by a human being with a
flashlight when exploring the dark undergrowth
(the episode that triggered Belinda's most recent
disappearance on a Caribbean island).

Spot responded to my call in Washington, but
only after two weeks. By then, the situation had
entirely changed, and he was desperate to get

home. Belinda did not respond at all, although she was probably within earshot all the time I was calling her. However, she came home during the night, hungry and smug.

As to where cats go when they put on a disappearing act—that remains a mystery at which one can only guess. My own suspicion is that they do not go far. I think they settle down in some snug hiding place, firmly closing their ears to their owners' urgent calling, until they decide that we have been punished enough for whatever we have done to upset them.

When a cat disappears, it is often impossible to tell whether it is pique or curiosity that has caused him to stray. When he returns, however, there is no doubt whatsoever.

A cat whose disappearance has been involuntary—that is, who has found himself shut up in a shed or has been chased up a tree by a dog—will arrive home in an intensely vocal mood. He will start off with a burst of righteous indignation, which will soon turn into an endless stream of information. He will go into great detail about his ordeal, explaining precisely what happened and demanding sympathy.

Conversely, a cat who has deliberately stayed away out of pique will return silently, usually at night. You will wake to find him sitting quietly on your bed, purring to indicate that the unpleasant incident is now closed, but sticking firmly to the old maxim of "never apologize; never explain."

If only one could be certain that every missing cat was just suffering from pique, one could wait calmly for him to get over his bad temper and come home. If only—

This brings us to the ever-present problem of whether or not to give your cats free rein if the environment is suitable. There is no easy answer. Certainly, if you keep your cats closely confined, you never have to worry about them getting lost or being stolen or run over. On the other hand, if you have once seen the sheer joy and exuberance of a cat who is free to run and hunt and climb and explore without restraint, it seems inhuman to deprive him of his happiness.

After much heart-searching, we have come down firmly on the side of freedom. If a disaster should one day occur, I feel that it is a calculated risk that we and the cats must all take; and I am convinced that if they had a say in the matter, they would agree.

It is worth remembering, too, that cats who are free to roam by themselves become very self-reliant and capable of getting out of scrapes on their own. They also develop a sense of self-preservation where automobile traffic is concerned, a proper caution when dealing with strange human beings, a good sense of direction, and an excellent homing instinct. These are all valuable protective skills. However, a cat who has been kept in and overcoddled by his owners finds himself thoroughly bewildered, disoriented, and unable to cope if he should accidentally stray or get lost.

I have noticed that our two cats, who are allowed the maximum free rein possible, behave with great intelligence and good sense when left on their own. For example, if we take them on a country picnic to a place that is strange to them, they will stay close to us at first. Then they will begin to explore the surrounding countryside cautiously, not letting us out of their sight and staying firmly together. When they are assured that we intend to remain in the same spot for some time, thus establishing a fixed headquarters, they will move farther afield and may go out of sight; but they stay together and come running at breakneck speed as soon as I call them.

They will behave in much the same way if we go to stay at an unfamiliar house or hotel, engaging in circumspect exploration and sticking together as a couple. However, once they become thoroughly accustomed to an environment, they invariably move off in different directions, each preferring to do his own thing in his own place. They only go in for teamwork when the terrain is unfamiliar, which seems to me to be eminently sensible.

In Chapter Nine, we will discuss environments and the best way in which to safeguard your pet and at the same time give him maximum freedom. Naturally, communication is absolutely vital if your cat is to be allowed to walk by himself. Yet again, it is a question of treating him as an intelligent creature, of teaching and encouraging him to use his brains and solve his own problems as far as possible.

In my experience, if cats are secure, happy, and in communication with their owners, they will not stray, except briefly in a fit of pique, no matter how much freedom they are given. They may be out of sight for quite long periods, but they seldom go out of earshot, and they will answer and come home if called.

This is an application of the same principle that

I discussed with regard to scraps from the dining table. The cat who knows he will get his treat later on is obedient and does not badger for food in the dining room. The cat who knows he is free to come and go is obedient and comes home when called. On the other hand, a pent-up cat who, following the impulse of his natural curiosity, escapes through an open door will most certainly not jeopardize his newfound freedom by returning in reply to a call. And by the time he wants to come home, he may well be thoroughly lost and incapable of coping with the situation.

The great majority of cats, however adventurous, always come home in the end unless prevented from doing so. There are certain cats, however, who make a habit of alternating between two or even more homes. This behavior is so uncatlike that I can only believe it is brought on by a deep sense of insecurity: I am the cat who is *forced* to walk by himself in order to survive. All places are alike to me, because I have no place of my own.

These cats are nearly always strays, and very attractive ones, too. One will arrive at your doorstep or windowsill, mewing piteously. You take him in and feed him and congratulate yourself on the fact that this charming cat has chosen *you* above all other people. The cat will be extremely affectionate, eat your food, and sleep on your bed.

The next day, the cat will still be there, and you will begin to take it for granted that this is your cat. A couple of days later, however, you arrive home in the evening with a fresh tin of food to find—no cat. Where can he be? Should you tell the police or the humane society? After all, he's not really your cat. Better forget it. He probably belongs to somebody else and just dropped in for a few days.

Just as you are successfully putting all thoughts of the cat out of your mind, he turns up again, every bit as hungry and affectionate but not starved by any means. And gradually a pattern emerges. It becomes obvious that he is spending Monday through Thursday elsewhere and Friday through Sunday with you. What are you going to do about it?

This depends entirely on how much you care about cats in general and this cat in particular. Although (as with humans) there are some unbalanced cats around who will behave in irrational ways, you can take it for granted that this cat is not crazy or greedy or superindependent. He is basically insecure.

Probably, he was once a well-cared-for domestic pet who has now been abandoned and become a stray. He may well have been picked up subsequently by a human family who thought him cute for a while, and then lost interest or moved away or ended their vacation and simply left him to fend for himself once more, feeling no sense of responsibility for him. Who can blame such a creature if he decides to hedge his bets and find not one but two establishments prepared to cater to his needs?

If you care seriously about him, then you must make a big effort. Use every means of communication with him, pet him and fondle him, talk to him and make him feel one of the family. If you don't really care much about him, cut down on the food, do not talk to him, and generally indicate that he is unwelcome. He will then either concentrate on the other home or find a substitute second snack bar. The sad thing is that such cats have become accustomed to rejection and regard a roving life as just a matter of survival.

To sum up, then, even the most faithful, loving, and communicative cats will occasionally disappear from home, either deliberately or because they are prevented from getting back.

It is a rare occurrence. Belinda is now nine years old, and Spot is eight. During those years, Spot has disappeared three times: once voluntarily, once involuntarily, and once (the two-week episode) a mixture of both. (These were absences of at least a day and a night, not his numerous hour-long sojourns in neighbors' garages.)

Belinda has also disappeared three times, and in each case it has been entirely deliberate. There was a fourth occasion, also deliberate, when she vanished from a beach in Portugal. But because we were some miles from our hotel, she had the sense to return after about four hours, just as we were packing up to leave, so that one doesn't real-

ly count. Belinda is a very smart cat. She is too
bright to get lost or trapped. Whatever she does is
done for a good reason. Like the proverbial English gentleman, she is never unintentionally
rude.

In the case of involuntary disappearances, the
personal vocal call sign is an indispensable
method of location and has a very high success
rate. Voluntary disappearances are a different
story.

Paradoxically, it is the highly intelligent loving,
communicating cats who have the character and
the brains to absent themselves out of pique. And
when they decide to do so, they are temporarily
deaf as adders when it comes to the call sign.
Hard though it may be, there is nothing to be
done but to trust in their common sense and ingenuity and wait for them to come back. In a way,
although it is difficult to persuade oneself of it at
the time, a deafening silence in response to your
call is actually encouraging. It probably means
that the little brute is safe and sound, well within
earshot, and determined to teach you a lesson in
order to redress some real or imagined wrong.
Best take the advice given to Little Bo-Peep.
"Leave them alone, and they'll come home . . ."

CHAPTER NINE

LIFESTYLES AND TRAVEL

When you acquire a cat or a kitten, you bring him into your environment; and whether he likes it or not, he must adapt to your lifestyle. Of course, a young kitten who grows up in your home accepts it as his natural ambience without question, but an older cat may take a little while to settle into your routine.

In my view, as expressed in Chapter Eight, cats should be given all the freedom possible so long as it is consistent with health and safety. Country cats are, of course, more fortunate than town cats in this respect; but even in the city, you can often work out a way of giving your cat fresh air and exercise.

There are apartment-dwelling cats who have literally never set foot outside. Their owners swear that they are perfectly happy, but to my mind the situation is far from ideal, and I would really not advise anybody to have a cat if it is to be imprisoned all its life. One thing is for certain. The only cat who can survive such an existence is one who has never known anything else, that is, a kitten brought up living indoors from the earliest age. It is easy enough to increase a cat's freedom, but it is out of the question to condemn a cat to apartment living if he has been accustomed to running free. However, the problem is not insoluble, as we shall see later.

Let us start, however, with the most fortunate of cats: the one whose owners live in the country, with a garden. He will be able to run free, to climb trees, and to hunt, as nature intended he should. If you love him and communicate well with him, you need not worry that he will stray voluntarily, at least not for long. But there are always the twin fears of a cat being lost or being stolen.

The first defense against these is to make sure that he *always* wears an identifying collar when out of doors. This collar should *not* be one made of leather or plastic with an identity disk in metal on it. Such collars should only be worn when traveling or walking the streets on a lead. Cats out on their own, whether in the city or the country, should wear the simplest and cheapest form of collar possible, a ring of ordinary 1/4-inch elastic with the cat's name, address, and phone number written on it in indelible ink. The reason for this is neither economy nor comfort, although both are secondary benefits, but the fact that an elastic collar eliminates the very real danger of accidental hanging. A free-roaming cat climbing a tree can get a leather or plastic collar caught on a twig, lose his footing, and hang himself. With an elastic collar, there is no risk of this because it fits his neck snugly. Also, as I said, these collars cost almost nothing, and the cat is scarcely aware that he has it on.

The cat living this idyllic life might be supposed to have no problems, and so long as his family stays put, this is true. However, nobody can predict his own future plans, and anyhow, there are vacations to be considered. The better the cat's environment, the less motivation there is to take steps to fit him for a different lifestyle. Without preparation, the shock, if it comes, is much harder to take. Therefore, I would urge owners of country cats to accustom their pets to travel and to take them on holiday (as I will describe later).

The next category is the suburban cat. He has his small garden and the possibility of a certain amount of freedom, but he also has the ever-present danger of automobile traffic, and he must learn to coexist with other cats on adjacent territories. It is particularly important for such a cat to develop a special cat-person call because he runs a real risk of getting locked in a shed or garage or otherwise finding himself prevented from getting

home; you must feel sure that you can always locate him by sound.

A suburban cat, or a town cat with access to a garden, is virtually certain to roam in neighboring gardens. There is really no fence or wall that an ingenious and active cat cannot scale. It is therefore very important to make sure that your neighbors do not object to seeing your cat in their gardens. If they have cats or dogs themselves, the problem is solved by the animals without trouble, for they all understand and respect territorial rights. But unfortunately, the people most likely to object are those who do not have pets of their own.

My own way of dealing with this situation is to get in touch with all my immediate neighbors in a new district before I let the cats out at all. I have been very lucky; nearly everybody has been kind and cooperative. If anybody seems dubious, I tell them that if they don't want the cats in their garden, the infallible way to get rid of them is to sprinkle some water on them. It does the cats no harm, but they loathe it and will very soon learn to stay away from that particular area.

Finally, we come to the city-dwelling cat, and he is the one with the greatest problems. If you are fortunate enough to have a small town garden, all the provisos that apply to the suburban cat also apply to yours, but even more intensely. The elastic collar, the cooperation of neighbors, and above all, the distinctive call and answer. What happens, though, if you live in an apartment or a town house with no garden, and you have no possibility of letting the cat go out?

For a start, you can teach your cat to walk on a lead or at least to ride on your shoulder. This process should be started very early in the kitten's life if it is to be successful. For walking, use a leather or plastic collar or, better still, a harness, and a lightweight lead. Make sure that the collar or harness is *not* elastic; if it is, the cat will easily escape. And make sure that it is tight enough to be escape-proof. Cats are very canny. My two Siamese quickly learned to puff themselves up while the harness was being put on, so that I was fooled into fastening it too loosely; then, once outside, they would turn to face me and back away, much

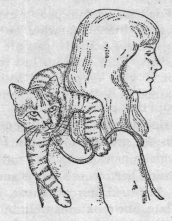

the easiest way to get out of a loose harness or collar.

A few cats take well and easily to walking on collar and lead, but, frankly, most of them hate it and never become entirely relaxed while out on the street. A good compromise is to put the collar and lead on the cat and then let him ride on your shoulder, which is probably one of his favorite perches anyhow. Naturally, you keep a firm hold on the lead, and this seems to give the cat a sense of security. He feels safe on his high roost and enjoys surveying the street scene. In this way, the cat can get some fresh air and take part in your life outside the apartment.

Far more important than an occasional airing is getting your cat accustomed to traveling by car so that he can go with you on holidays and for country weekends. For some reason, people expect dogs to travel with their human families but are surprised when cats do so. Actually, cats are far more portable than dogs. They take up less room and, from the point of view of personal hygiene, are quite self-contained and do not need constant exercising outside.

The sooner the process of accustoming your cat to car travel begins, the better. Belinda was four months old when she came to us, and she had never been outside her owner's house and garden. Consequently, her training as a car passenger started rather late. She took to it well, but she still sometimes shows signs of agitation after four or five hours of a really long journey.

On the other hand, when she had her kittens, the whole family came in the car with us even before the kittens' eyes were opened. As a result, Spot regards the car as a natural part of his life and thoroughly enjoys journeys. However, you do have to keep your cat in practice for car riding. Some of Spot's brothers and sisters, who had the advantage of the same early training that he did, went to homes where they do little or no traveling and are now reported to have reverted to being neurotic yowlers who have had to learn all over again how to be tranquil and competent travelers.

Here are a few useful pointers for travel by car. Provide a good, comfortable cat carrier lined with toweling or a blanket, and always use it for carrying the cats to and from the car. If you are driving

alone with your cats, it is better to leave them in the carrier throughout the trip, although I must confess to breaking this rule myself on occasion. If there are two or more of you, however, you can let the cats out of the carrier on collars and leads to sit on the lap of the passenger. They love this, staring eagerly out of the window to observe the passing scene.

On a long journey (three hours or more) when the cats can be let out of their carrier, we have found it an excellent idea to provide a box of cat litter on the floor at the back of the car. After a little while on the road, there is always a sound of satisfied scrabbling, and it seems to give the cats a great sense of security to know that their box is available. They are much too clean to foul the car and much to scared to perform if taken out for roadside stops. The whole cat-box question can give rise to worries and anxieties on long trips if you do not provide one as I have suggested.

Food is a different matter. I always bring food and water for my cats, but I have found that it is very unusual for them to eat or drink en route. Probably, they are just too excited.

Once cats have become thoroughly used to traveling by car, it is a short and easy step to introduce them to trains and planes (and, in our case, small sailing boats). So long as they are constantly reassured of your presence, and so long as you keep talking to them and explaining what is happening, they will relish every new experience.

Apropos of air travel, please *never* allow your pet to travel in the baggage compartment. Despite what the airlines may say in their publicity, these compartments can suffer extremes of heat and cold, let alone lack of proper pressurization, and pets have been known to arrive dead, after unimaginable suffering. It is quite simple, as a rule, to take your cat or cats in the cabin with you, just so long as you make the arrangements far enough ahead and get the permission of the airline. When it comes to airlines, they vary.

I shall never forget my first experience of flying on my own with the cats from Geneva to New York. We were booked on Swissair, and I had made arrangements ahead of time, of course, to bring the cats into the cabin with me. However, I was only too prepared for snags to develop. Consequently, when my name was called on the airport broadcast system to report to the Swissair desk, I went along with the worst forebodings. Something had obviously gone wrong, I thought, and there was going to be trouble about the cats. I was going to be told that they must travel in the baggage compartment after all.

Well, I wasn't going to have it. I am easily intimidated as a rule, but where the cats are concerned, I become a veritable tigress. I was going to stand up to the ridiculous bureaucracy of the airline. I was going to refuse point-blank to travel without the cats in the cabin. I was prepared to take the issue to the highest court in the land. I was—

I arrived at the desk furious and bursting with adrenaline, my scathing reply already formulated. The girl said, "Ah, madame. You are the lady with the cats?"

"Yes, I am, and if you think you can—"

"We are so delighted to welcome you aboard, madame. Would you care to choose your seat ahead of the other passengers, so that the cats may be comfortable? Then we would like you to board before the others, so that you may get settled in. And the purser has asked if the cats would like any special sort of food or drink during the voyage, so that he may prepare it."

I felt exactly as if I had stepped on a stair that

wasn't there. For a couple of seconds, I couldn't do anything but open and shut my mouth silently, like a goldfish. Then I managed to say, "Thank you."

That was the first experience, and it has been followed by many others, equally heartwarming. So I say again, "Thank you, Swissair."

On international flights, animals (and their carriers) are weighed and charged as excess baggage, irrespective of how much or little actual baggage you may have. Your cat will always need a recent health certificate from a qualified veterinarian and a certificate of valid inoculation against rabies. The important thing is to find out the policies of various airlines with regard to animals.

These vary from the wonderful tolerance of Swissair to the inflexible hostility of British Airways, who will never allow any animal in any passenger cabin under any circumstances. In between, each airline has its own rules, and you or your travel agent will have to be really persistent about finding them out, because they are subject to change and not every reservation clerk has the latest information at his fingertips. If your cat is accepted as a passenger, it is advisable to ask for written confirmation of his booking, just in case anything should go wrong.

The attitude of British Airways is, of course, explained by the Draconian quarantine regulations of the United Kingdon, which make it impossible for British people to take their animals on holidays abroad, or for foreign visitors to bring theirs in, so that the question of transport for domestic pets simply does not arise. However, it is possible to take cats through London Airport in transit, as we well know.

When we finally uprooted our household from Europe to the United States, it was necessary for various reasons that we should be routed from Geneva via London to Washington, D.C. Naturally, the cats would be with us.

We made every possible arrangement in advance, and the British agreed that we might take the cats in transit through London so long as neither of them sullied British soil by setting paw beyond the customs area. All well and good. We disembarked from the Geneva plane and made our way towards the transit lounge. I was carrying the two cats in their wicker basket, and Jim toted the rest of our hand luggage.

It was quite a long walk, and just outside the lounge, I decided to rest my arm for a moment by putting the cat carrier down on the ground. As I was about to do so, a voice with an unmistakably constabulary ring to it said, "Hey!"

I looked up, alarmed, to see an enormous policeman, complete with motorcycle, looming over me. He said, "Cats in there?"

"Yes."

"Ar. Don't put the basket on the ground. Shouldn't 'ave come this far. I've come to collect 'em."

"To what?"

"Take 'em to the quarantine area."

"All right," I said. "Let's go."

The policeman did not seem to understand. He said, "I've come to take the cats."

Firmly, I replied, "Where the cats go, I go."

"Oh, no, madam. That's not allowed."

"I don't care what's allowed. If the cats can go to this quarantine area, then so can I. I'm not leaving them."

The policeman then made a fatal error in psychology. He said, soothingly, "I don't think you'd much like it over there, madam. It's rather cold and dank, if you know what I mean. And here you've got this lovely warm transit lounge—"

"In that case," I yelled, "*nothing* will persuade me to part with my cats!"

He saw his mistake at once and backpedaled. "Well, now, madam—that's not to say it's cold. Not really cold. Not for the animals. Very snug, they are."

Jim was beginning to assume the cross, embarrassed expression that I call his "for heaven's sake" look. He said, "For heaven's sake, Penny, the officer is simply saying that it's against the rules for you to go there. Isn't that right?"

"Yes, sir," said the policeman gratefully, and he added, with a burst of inspiration, "It'll be nicer for them, see, madam? They'll be able to come out of their box and have a meal and—"

Even Jim protested at that. "Good God, man, if

you let them out of their carrier in a strange place, with neither of us there, you'll never catch them again. And they're not supposed to be fed during the journey."

"Very well, sir." There was a pause, and then the unfortunate officer at last found the right thing to say. It was: "After all, madam, it's only for an hour."

I began to feel a little silly. Only for an hour. I said, "All right. I suppose you'd better take them." In any case, my right arm was about to break from keeping the box off England's green and pleasant land.

"Thank you, madam." Obviously relieved, the policeman loaded the cat carrier onto the back of his motorcycle and roared away with two small, indignant faces glaring at me through the bars of the cage. Jim and I went off to get a drink.

Three-quarters of an hour later, the loud-speaker made its inevitable announcement: "Pan American Airways regrets to announce a delay in the departure of their flight to Washington. A further announcement will be made as soon as possible."

In fact, three further announcements were made, and it was five hours later that a relieved loudspeaker was able to request that all passengers on the Pan American flight to Washington should proceed to gate number something for immediate boarding.

At the gate, nobody knew anything about any

cats. The flight was already very late, and every-body was asked to board with all possible speed. I began to shout. I was *not* going to get on that air-craft and fly off to America, leaving my cats in a cold, dank quarantine area with instructions that they were not to be fed.

Jim went into an even bigger "for heaven's sake." "People are meeting us at the other end," he thundered. "We've *got* to be on this plane."

Kicking and screaming, I was dragged aboard. The hostess was charming and unflappable and in-furiating. "I'm sure everything will be just fine," she said smilingly, as she prepared to shut the door of the Boeing 747.

And then, in the distance, I heard the sound of a police siren. I ran to the door to see a motor-cycle outrider speeding across the tarmac, fol-lowed by a huge black police limousine with siren blaring and lights flashing. The convoy screamed to a halt beside the jumbo jet. The motorcyclist jumped off his machine and opened the door of the limousine. From the back seat, with some cere-mony, he extracted the wicker cat basket, from which peered two wide-eyed and very scared little faces. The basket was put aboard just as the great doors slammed shut, and the aircraft taxied off to her takeoff point. Once again, England had been made safe for democracy and uninoculated ani-mals.

As a matter of fact, that journey marked a high point in Belinda's life. An inveterate snob, on pre-

vious flights she had resolutely tried to escape from the economy section into the first-class cabin, where she obviously felt that she belonged. On this particular trip, Jim's employers had generously provided us with first-class tickets, and so Belinda found herself not only traveling first class at last, but on a 747, with that lovely spiral staircase and upstairs bar and separate dining room and all. Furthermore, several of the flight crew, including the captain himself, came aft from the cockpit to talk to the cats. Never before nor since has Belinda been so much the grande dame, nor has she enjoyed herself so thoroughly, except perhaps for the time when she was accommodated in the eighteenth-century papal suite of a converted Portuguese monastery.

However, back to earth.

I cannot overemphasize that the secret of traveling with a quiet, contented cat rather than a protesting screecher lies in explaining in advance to the cat just where you and he are going and what is happening. I cannot imagine that you yourself would relish being unceremoniously uprooted from a quiet routine of life, rammed into a small basket, and carted off to noisy and unfamiliar places, all without a word of explanation. Well, your cat feels just the same way that you do.

Your intention of going on a journey will be clearly signaled to the cat by the appearance of suitcases and the bustle of packing. If he is accustomed to going with you, he will be highly delighted at the prospect. My cats are not the only ones I know who pack themselves by sitting firmly in the open suitcases to make sure they will not be left behind. However, if the cat does not as a rule accompany you, the appearance of the suitcases will make him very melancholic because he will realize that you are about to leave him.

If you are taking your cat with you, explain to him where you are going, by what form of transportation, and how long the journey will take. It may sound fanciful, but I can assure you that cats are much better behaved and more patient on a long and perhaps uncomfortable journey if they have been briefed in advance about it.

If they have been promised a quick, convenient trip, and then bad weather or mechanical breakdown turns it into a lengthy and frustrating one, they get pretty cross. Only grudgingly will they accept your explanation that it really is not your fault.

On the other hand, I have found that in a genuine emergency, they behave in an exemplary manner. On one horrible occasion, Jim and I were driving home to Holland from Switzerland along a German autobahn when we were crashed into from behind by a driver who had evidently succumbed to motorway monotony and failed to notice the traffic jam ahead that had caused us to slow down. Fortunately, our car was an extremely strong one, with plenty of solid metal between the front-seat passengers and the rear bumper. All the same, the violence of the impact detached both front seats from their moorings and buckled the doors, trapping us inside temporarily. The cats, who were on my lap in the passenger seat, were thrown onto the floor and under the seat, which shot forward over them.

It was a long and dreary business. First, we had to be extracted from the car. Then came police formalities. Finally, the car was towed away to a nearby garage, where we waited for hours while mechanics contrived to get it into a condition in which it could be driven home, but at no more than about fifteen miles an hour. We had several hundred miles to do at this grindingly low speed.

The accident happened at three o'clock in the afternoon, and we finally got home at about two o'clock in the morning.

Through all this, the cats never complained once. They stayed very close to me, occasionally licking my hand for mutual reassurance. There were no protests, no caterwaul, nothing to make an already unpleasant situation worse. They obviously realized that it had not been our fault, that we were as upset and shocked as they were, and that we were doing all we could to set matters right. I was greatly impressed by their behavior, because they are a strong-willed and demanding couple, and as a rule, they would have made a great fuss about the delay and discomfort.

No matter how much you travel with your cat, there are bound to be trips on which you cannot take him, such as business journeys or visits to countries with quarantine regulations. It is especially important on those occasions to explain to the cat as soon as the suitcases are brought out that this time he must stay at home. He will be bitterly disappointed, of course, and possibly resentful, but it is much better and kinder to make it clear to him right away rather than allow him to get excited at the prospect of a trip and then simply walk out on him.

When you must leave him behind, the question arises of what arrangements to make for him. I am prepared to leave my cats alone in the house for up to four days with a neighbor coming in twice a day to feed them; but for a longer period, this is not a satisfactory solution unless you can be sure that the person feeding the cat is a real friend of his and is prepared to spend time each day talking to him and playing with him.

Even that is not an ideal arrangement. A little while ago, I acted as cat-sitter to a beautiful black-and-white cat whose family had to go away for three weeks and who thought it was better for him to stay at home rather than be boarded out in a cattery. Of course, I knew the cat well, and I spent at least half an hour every day with him (as I mentioned earlier, he taught me several new games). Nevertheless, after about ten days he began to show signs of real distress. When I prepared to leave him, he would stand on his hind legs and clasp my leg in his arms, begging me not to go; and as I went out through the front door, I was unhappily aware of the drooping tail, the depressed ears, and the big, reproachful green eyes. He survived, of course, and is none the worse now, but I was very glad when his owners came home.

On the other hand, I doubt if he would have been better off in a cattery, for cats are intensely attached to places as well as to people. The ideal thing is to find somebody who is prepared to live in your house and look after your cat while you are away. I know that such people are not easy to find, but it is worthwhile to make a real effort. It goes without saying that it must be somebody who is a true cat lover, prepared to give your animal the same sort of affection to which he is accustomed.

Much the best, naturally, is to take the cat with you. In our family, the cats' traveling needs are packed in a medium-sized zip-up bag, and consist of:

> tins of cat food, 2 per day of the journey, plus 1 in reserve
> plastic bag of cat biscuits (very convenient for in-transit snacks)
> 2 plates
> water bottle
> water dish
> folding cardboard cat boxes
> cat box liners
> cat-box litter, enough for a clean box each day of journey
> tin opener
> medium-size plastic garbage bags
> paper towels
> 1 knife
> 1 spoon

When I specify *the journey*, I mean actual traveling time, not the whole length of the holiday. I count on being able to buy food and cat litter wherever we go, but I do take a couple of spare folding cat boxes as a reserve because they are not available everywhere. With this equipment, your cat or cats can be completely independent and cause no bother to anybody, either en route or at a hotel.

Once again, it is most important to prearrange with the hotel to make sure the cat will be welcome. It is *not* advisable to turn up with an unannounced cat and risk being refused admission. If our plans are so uncertain that it is impossible to book ahead, I consult the hotel guide and avoid those establishments that display the No Dogs symbol (a cat is not a dog, and one might win on a legal technicality, but I am not prepared to risk it.) Then I always try to telephone in advance, even if it is only a few hours before arrival.

Once you have arrived at the hotel, set up a cat headquarters in the bathroom if you have a private one, otherwise in a corner of the bedroom. In the latter case, it is a good idea to spread newspaper on the floor under the cat box and dishes. Put down the cat box with its plastic liner and a sufficient but not overgenerous filling of cat litter. Open a tin of cat food, spoon it onto the plate, and fill the water dish. Your cat will now be perfectly equipped and happy for his overnight stay. (I am taking it for granted that the cat will sleep on your bed).

In the morning, after the cat has been fed, put the cat-box liner, complete with soiled litter, into a plastic garbage bag, together with the empty tins of food. Tie the garbage bag securely, and put it into the wastepaper basket. Wash the dishes and dry them on paper towels. Refold the cardboard cat box and pack it, together with the other equipment. There will be no trace that a cat has ever occupied the room. We have used this technique all over the world and have never had a single complaint, either from the hotel management or from other guests.

Here, then, in summary, are the rules for traveling with cats:

1. Make all arrangements well ahead of time.
2. Find out the exact regulations concerning cats as applied by the airline, railway, or other carrier you are using.
3. Tell the cat your plans in detail before you leave.
4. Pack everything necessary, but do not bloat your luggage with inessentials.

Bon voyage!

CHAPTER TEN

IN CONCLUSION

This may appear to be a lighthearted and even frivolous book, and in so far as this makes it entertaining and easy to read, I am glad that it should be considered so. In fact, though, the underlying premise is serious and not unscholarly.

The cat as a highly intelligent and communicating creature is being studied and observed in considerable depth these days, and many things are being learned by scientists about his behavior that any alert and loving cat owner could have told them years ago. It is an excellent step in the right direction, however, that these truths should be given the stamp of academic respectability. The murk of the Dark Ages is at last being dispersed officially, and it is no longer necessary to apologize self-deprecatingly for admiring and communicating with cats.

Since I began to write this book, I have talked to numerous and diverse people about their cats, and I have found that communication between human beings and cats exists everywhere. People are just wary of talking too much about it for fear of ridicule.

I have been told of many personal call signs between cats and people, including one in which the human call was a high-pitched whistle. This is obviously a very sensible idea because a whistle carries farther than a cry, and in fact the owner used it to locate a cat that had been lost for eight days in a New Hampshire forest.

Each owner who has evolved the personal call-sign-and-reply method seems to think that he or she is the only person ever to have done it. I admit that I used to think that I was. The usual reaction is, "Well, I hardly like to talk about it. People would laugh."

I have also heard of communicating cats who have an apparently uncanny ability to predict exactly when an absent owner will return home. On the morning of the appointed day, the cat becomes excited, paces about by the front door, or remains glued to a windowpane, watching for the car. When pressed, the owner admits, sheepishly, "Yes, of course I told him when I'd be coming back. I always do. But who is going to believe that he really understands what I say to him?"

Observation of cat colonies has also turned up interesting results. I have already touched on the extramural experiments conducted by Dr. Lucile St. Hoyme, Associate Curator of Physical Anthropology at the Smithsonian Institute in Washington, D.C. I have been privileged to talk to her about her work and to see her photographs, and I hope that her paper on the experiment will appear soon.

Dr. St. Hoyme's observation of a large group of cats in protected conditions is backed up by the less scientific but intensely empirical experience of Barbara Jamieson. Barbara, married to a doctor and mother of a teen-age family, is a living refutation of the idea that to be absorbed by cats one must be slightly crazy, dowdy, eccentric, and/or a frustrated spinster. She is extremely pretty, petite, and chic. All the same, she and her husband (who fully shares her enthusiasm) never have fewer that fifty cats in their home.

They take in the hopeless cases, the cats that are not cute, the cats that nobody else wants. At the moment of writing, they have a spastic tabby who has little control over his back legs but gets around very well nonetheless and who, in the communicative atmosphere of the Jamieson home, has blossomed into a charming personality. They have a cat who lost both front legs above the paws as the result of an accident. They have two cats who are blind in one eye. They take in the scared and the unloved, as well as offering a home to happy, integrated cats whose owners, for one reason or another, simply cannot keep them.

The most striking thing about the Jamieson colony is the complete harmony in which the cats live together. Barbara isolates a newcomer for a day or so and then introduces him gradually to the others, and she stresses communication as the most important factor. She explains to the other cats, and they understand. Only in one particular does she disagree with my conclusion in this book, and that is the fact that, in her very wide experience, it is the females who use more vocal talk than the males. Spot and Belinda, I presume, must be the exceptions that prove the rule.

There is one big difference between the Jamieson and the St. Hoyme colonies. Cats taken in by the Jamiesons are always spayed or neutered on arrival if this has not already been done: whereas Dr. St. Hoyme wished to observe unaltered cats going about their natural processes of forming couples and family groups.

Both colonies demonstrate that cats can and do live harmoniously with each other when the conditions are right, that is, when there is human affection and communication and no stress in the matter of food and shelter. The St. Hoyme cats formed monogamous couples, and the various females with kittens baby-sat for each other; even the tomcats took their turns at caring for the kittens. The Jamieson cats welcome newcomers without fuss and demonstrate great friendship towards

each other, and all join in the general atmosphere of human love and communication.

Cats are by now too domesticated by breeding to lead a satisfactory existence without human aid and care. Alley cats survive, to be sure; but they lose their true catliness, just as all but the most remarkable people are dehumanized by intolerable living conditions. However, they (the alley cats) can quickly be restored to full cathood by adoption into a human family, love, care, and communication. People who have mounted rescue operations for the so-called wild cats (not truly wild, of course, but domestic cats that have been abandoned) in Venice, Rome, and London report that at the first human contact the cats begin to respond and to communicate and that after a short while they are ready for adoption, unless, of course, they are in such desperate physical condition that there is no solution except to destroy them painlessly.

A friend of mine who does this work in London recently found a colony of abandoned cats in the dock area, all of whom were so ill, wounded, or starving as to make rehabilitation impossible. She, like the Jamiesons, takes in and cares for any cat that can be nursed back to health. But in this case, there was absolutely nothing to be done but to catch the cats and take them to the veterinarian for euthanasia.

She reports that, heartbreakingly, they became calm and happy when put into cat carriers and licked her hand in gratitude on their way to the death chamber. "There was nothing else I could do for them," she said, "but at least they seemed to know that at last somebody cared what happened to them and was not prepared to leave them in their misery."

The operative word in that last sentence is *somebody*. We have brought it upon ourselves by striking that original, prehistoric bargain: food, warmth, and affection in return for a clean, healthy, rodent-free home. Rudyard Kipling was not wrong about that, I am sure. What he did get wrong was the idea that the cats also regarded it as a bargain and decided nevertheless to walk by themselves. Cats hunt rats and mice for sport. Do not imagine that they are doing us a favor by so doing. They accept our friendship joyously, thinking it to be freely given, as is theirs to us, a mutual demonstration of affection between intelligent creatures, with no strings attached, involving spontaneous love and loyalty. Too often, they are disappointed.

In the beginning, people needed cats more than cats needed people. There was no other practical way of solving the rodent problem (the Pied Piper of Hamelin was never paid, took his revenge, and did not offer his services again). Nowadays, man has invented poisons and pesticides and can manage without the cat. But over the centuries, the cat has come to rely on us and now cannot do without us. The time has come to forget the bargain and instead to enjoy the unique opportunity for genuine friendship with an animal.

The time has come to communicate. Many people are already doing so. Others regard the cat as an ornament, a symbol of cozy domesticity, or just as a nuisance that their children insisted on bringing home. I would ask these people to reconsider, to reevaluate their pet in terms of a communicating entity and a member of the household. They will find it well worthwhile.

It is very simple. Talk to your cat, and he will talk to you.

ABOUT THE AUTHOR

Patricia Moyes is the author of thirteen mysteries. She recently moved with her husband and their two Siamese cats, Spot and Belinda, to Virgin Garda, one of the British Virgin Islands.

SIGNET Books of Special Interest

**Buy them at your local
bookstore or use coupon
on next page for ordering.**

SIGNET Books of Related Interest

(0451)

☐ **HOUSE PLANTS FOR FIVE EXPOSURES by George Taloumis.** The complete guide to lighting—and living with—your plants. Illustrated with many photographs, this book offers hundreds of ways to make your indoor greenery flourish like the great outdoors.
(119223—$2.50)*

☐ **THE APARTMENT GARDENER by Florence and Stanley Dworkin.** The total guide to indoor planting that will tell you how to pick plants that grow beautifully indoors, when water is your plant's worst enemy, all about those plants that love to hide in dimly lighted corners, raising plants from pits and seeds, and hundreds of other plant-growing and protecting tips that can put a little bit of the country into apartment living.
(084144—$1.75)

☐ **THE GREENHOUSE GARDENER by Elvin McDonald.** This completely revised, updated, and expanded version of *The Flowering Greenhouse Day by Day* is the complete homeowner and apartment dweller's guide to glassed-in gardening. Profusely illustrated.
(090373—$1.75)

☐ **THE ROCKWELLS' COMPLETE GUIDE TO SUCCESSFUL GARDENING by F. F. Rockwell and Esther C. Grayson.** Everything you need to know from planning home grounds to planting and maintaining them, including a handy calendar guide and a region guide based on the growing season from the winners of the Citation for Horticultural Achievement of the American Horticultural Society.
(097432—$3.95)

*Prices slightly higher in Canada

Buy them at your local bookstore or use this convenient coupon for ordering.

THE NEW AMERICAN LIBRARY, INC.,
P.O. Box 999, Bergenfield, New Jersey 07621

Please send me the books I have checked above. I am enclosing $_____
(please add $1.00 to this order to cover postage and handling). Send check or money order—no cash or C.O.D.'s. Prices and numbers are subject to change without notice.

Name_____

Address_____

City _____ State _____ Zip Code _____
Allow 4-6 weeks for delivery.
This offer is subject to withdrawal without notice.

The Best in Fiction from SIGNET

(0451)

*Price slightly higher in Canada.

Buy them at your local
bookstore or use coupon
on next page for ordering.

Great Reading from SIGNET